Foreword

This year, the Young Writers' 'Poetry In Motion' competition proudly presents a showcase of the best poetic talent selected from over 40,000 up-and-coming writers nationwide.

Young Writers was established in 1991 to promote the reading and writing of poetry within schools and to the youth of today. Our books nurture and inspire confidence in the ability of young writers and provide a snapshot of poems written in schools and at home by budding poets of the future.

The thought effort, imagination and hard work put into each poem impressed us all and the task of selecting poems was a difficult but nevertheless enjoyable experience.

We hope you are as pleased as we are with the final selection and that you and your family continue to be entertained with *Poetry In Motion Bristol* for many years to come.

GW00640688

Poetry In Motion

Bristol

Edited by Steve Twelvetree

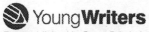 Young**Writers**

First published in Great Britain in 2004 by:
Young Writers
Remus House
Coltsfoot Drive
Peterborough
PE2 9JX
Telephone: 01733 890066
Website: www.youngwriters.co.uk

SB ISBN 1 84460 393 8

Contents

Sarah Vernon (13)   72
Florence McClelland (13)   72
Carla Ahmadi (13)   73
Imogen Small (13)   73
Christine Vien (13)   74
Alys Fletcher (13)   75
Alex Bartlett (13)   76
Elena Gugunava (13)   76
Emma Hatton (13)   77
Naomi Holloway (13)   77
Hattie Lister (13)   78
Katie White (13)   78
Natalie Parker (13)   79
Megan Pardoe (14)   79
Jade Jetley (14)   80
Elizabeth Evans (13)   80
Charlotte Lonsdale (13)   81
Stephanie Kelley (14)   81
Sharon Mundozo (14)   82
Saliha Mahmood (14)   83
Jane Holmes (13)   84
Hannah Hoskins (14)   85
Anoushka Campbell (14)   86
Lucy Webber (14)   87

Filton High School
Joseph Hamlen (11)   88
Gurveet Singarda (11)   88
David Dolan (11)   89
Melanie Chapman (11)   89
Rebecca Collins (11)   90
James Roe (11)   90
Catherine Bailey (12)   91
Amy Smurthwaite (11)   91
Roxanne Perkins (11)   92
Tom Williamson (11)   92
Rahat Ahmed (11)   93
David Stafford (13)   93
Amy Dunning (11)   94
Connor Coles (11)   94
Chris Lewin (11)   95

Najwa Bassir (11)	95
Lauren Nutt (11)	96
Richard Higbey (11)	96
Amy Wakeford (11)	97
Christopher Wide (11)	97
Rachael Nicholls (11)	98
Hazel Gowen (11)	98
Jason Dixon (11)	99
Matthew Cooper (11)	99
Sammy Mountford (11)	100
Ben Turner (11)	100
Hayley Clifford (12)	101
Jack Rice (11)	101
Sophie Vardon (12)	102
Mack Johnson (11)	102
Matthew Grey (11)	103
Shauna Brain (11)	103
Naomi Jones (12)	104
Katie Leck (11)	104
Jamie Mitchell (12)	105
Kai Smith (11)	105
Chris Winstone (11)	106
Abigail Chodkiewicz (11)	106
Jade Weston (11)	106
Gethyn Ulyatt (11)	107
Alex Leggett (11)	107
Diana Sakota (11)	107
Adam Gleeson (11)	108
Adam Turner (11)	108
Steven Mitchell (11)	109
David McCann (11)	109
Danny Reed (11)	110
Michael Rowsell (11)	110
James Ashdown (11)	111
Jessica Andrews (11)	111
Morgane Foster (11)	112
Jordan Estcourt (12)	112
Jyothi Pillay (12)	113
Shelly Janes (11)	113
Natasha Cameron (12)	114
Charlotte Done (11)	114
Rebecca Dale (12)	115

Emil Lowenberg (12) 210
Rhiannon Stoate (12) 211
Becca North (13) 212
Louis Osborne (12) 213
Sarah Huckle (12) 214
Sam Baker (13) 215
Laura Smith (13) 216
Thomas Andrews (13) 217
Bobbie-Ann Poulton (12) 218
Matthew Hooper (12) 219
Martin Hutton (12) 220
Alice Byrne (12) 221
Heather Sinclair (12) 222
Patrick Lines (12) 223
Rachel Kwok (12) 224
Sarah Galsworthy (13) 225
Sam Hunt (12) 226
Nick Krupa (12) 227
Victoria Piper (14) 228
Gregory Vardon-Smith (13) 229

Warmley Park Special School
Jessica Watts (13) 229

The Poems

Is Life A Game?

I sit at the corner watching
People chasing, running and marking
I normally think life is just a game
There are plenty of experiences to gain
You have your teammates on your side
So you must have some friends nearby
But what if they aren't *really* there?
If it's just imagination in my head?

One of my teammates tripped, is she okay
Or is she trying to help the other team to play?
'Shoot! Shoot!' everyone screams
She has the best position but she misses
'Oh well! Bad luck,' the coach says
So I have to take her place instead
I stand outside the line
The truth I see I try to deny
Suddenly I see I *am* the only one
The sweat in my hand starts to run
I hold onto the ball tightly
When the referee blows the whistle loudly
I look to see who to pass to
I realise I am the only blue . . .
Wait a minute, why is that?
Everyone here is wearing red,
I chuck the ball to my so-called team
Running fast, I can hardly see . . .
Who did I pass the ball to? I think,
Sweat running down my eye, I blink,
I can't take this anymore
I scream and I fall to the floor.

Cynthia Fong (15)
Badminton School

The Joker

He was the man with no name,
His goal to reach the perfect fame.
He was the hero, the bait,
No one but them, knew his oblique fate.

The prying birds flew away,
Even the Devil stopped its dirty play.
But yet he served his purpose,
Like a bloody circus.

With no regret or shame
They surely gave him the perfect fame.
In their ecstasy of lust,
They completed their filthy tricks.

William Lord (15)
Bristol Grammar School

The Poor Farmer

The sun shines fiercely on the dry ground
Nothing can escape the sun's bright rays
Wherever you look, no one is moving around
The trees are shimmering, in the midday haze.

The birds are hiding amongst the leaves
The animals resting in the shade of trees
People at home, keeping themselves cool
Saying anyone outside today must be a fool.

In the fields stands a lone man
Ploughing the ground with all his might
Cleaning sweat off his face with a wave of his hand
Working until the day turns to night.

As evening comes he leaves to rest
Working today has been a real test
Why has he been working in the sun's full glare?
He doesn't have a choice, so he doesn't really care.

Mohammad Rashiq Sharif (14)
Bristol Grammar School

War

Gas flooding,
People dying,
Bunkers blowing,
People going sky-high,
Shouting, screaming,
Everywhere,
Guns going *bang, bang!*
Soldiers marching,
Tank attacking,
Aeroplanes flying,
With big tears dropping,
Landmines blowing.
Bushes burning
People tripping over barbed wire,
Blood squirting everywhere,
I *hate* war.

Tanzil Ahmed (15)
Bristol Grammar School

The Scroungers

Everything's locked and there's nowhere to go,
The Scroungers strike back with their profile so low.

They perch behind park benches just waiting to pounce,
With eyes on the lookout, ready to scare but an ounce -
Of your trembling body, a block of shivering ice,
As they reach for their daggers to cut just a slice -
Of that fresh-looking child, whose cold, slender meat,
Will be served on a plate and ready to eat.

So children beware,
Never go alone at night,
Where Scroungers may lay,
Ready to give you a fright.

Jenny Cross (14)
Bristol Grammar School

Lost And Found

'I've lost my what and my thing,
I can't find my whatsymajig,
its skin was scaly and its name was Maney
and its figure was stumpy and big.'

'What about a snake or a sheep,
a sandwich or even a swan?
A sack or your sock, a shop or a shock,
a sweet or even a song?'

'No!' I cried and I shouted, 'it's none of them I'm sure,
but I think you're close, apart from your boast,
I think it just fell on the floor.'

'Is it your shirt or a salmon,
your smile or even your sweets?
But whatever it is, the creature sounds big,
so I'll stop and have something to eat.'

Whilst I sat and ate up my food,
I noticed something quite crude,
daring to ask what my mother had cooked,
when my father burst in and was rude.

'What have you eaten, you vile-smelling snob,
it smells like you've eaten our pedigree dog.
You smell like that sausage, no wait, that's a spot
now go quickly and have a shower and sop!'

Whilst my mother was gone to the shower,
I noticed quite clearly, the power.
'The spanner, the spanner, the spanner,' I cried.
'The spanner, will be burnt and scorched alive.'

I went upstairs, the bathroom was misty,
but I noticed the spanner revived and bewildered.

Rebecca Fellows (15)
Bristol Grammar School

The Wood

Walking slowly through the wood,
the time has come I knew it should.
No birds to hear my heavy breath,
no harbinger of the death.

The misty dew will fall so soon,
my footsteps lit by just the moon.
Crunch! The twigs beneath my feet,
just like my bones with fear do creak.

The monster approaches, I knew he would,
to surprise him now I wish I could.
I bide my time, I stop and stare,
I see his face, his evil glare.

His gang has left him on his own,
the bully finds his own way home.
Through the woods his path does take,
I follow closely in his wake.

I pounce and bring him to the floor,
that's it. It's started. We're at war.
I grab the blade and raise it high,
hoping, hoping he would cry.

I wanted to just scare him stiff,
he was always meant to live.
He had beat me, bruised me, made me lie,
I just wanted him to cry.

The boy is dead, they asked me: How?
But just who is the bully now?

Christopher Cross (15)
Bristol Grammar School

Man Catching Fish

This is a story about a man and a fish,
the man wants to see the fish dead in a dish,
He wants to eat him with lemon and chips,
he'll gobble him up whilst smacking his lips.

The man's name is Fish-eye Jones, he's so excited,
all his friends he phoned,
'Gilbert, Edwina, Freddy and Bob,
today's the day I catch the cod.'

But Fishy McDishy - not scared he might die,
said, 'You go on matey, just give it a try!'
But Fishy McDishy was wondering why,
his friend Fish-eye Jones wanted him in a pie.

Jones said he'd catch him in April some time,
he'd go down to the beach when the weather was fine,
The spectators gathered and Jones took his rod,
he used rotten maggots for bait, which was odd.

He cast out his line and anticipated,
a tug, or a pull - but five hours they waited,
But just as Jones thought he'd pack up and leave,
from the end of the line came a wonderful heave!

Stricken with panic he was swept off his feet,
with his head in his maggots he was dragged down the beach,
The crowd made a roar as Jones took a spin,
cos Fishy McDishy had pulled him right in!

The crowd listened up, as Bob made a shout,
'I wonder if Jonesey will ever come out?'
The crowd gasped in horror as Jones disappeared,
'Don't worry about Jonesey,' said a man with a beard.

'Good gosh, he's a goner,' another man sneered,
but then, in the distance, something appeared.
The poor Fish-eye Jones, with his face going red,
was held by McDishy, high above his head!

He walked up the beach for all to see,
the crowd really loved him - a celeb-rity,
They weighed poor old Fish-eye, all dripping and wet,
then Fishy McDishy said, 'My best catch yet!'

Andy Lowe (15)
Bristol Grammar School

Football

The football season is under way
Who will win the Premiership title?
No one will dare say
To every team this trophy is vital

Arsenal, Man U and Liverpool are all contenders
But which of these is the best?
Chelsea are the league's big spenders
But will they be better than the rest?

Can any team beat Arsenal and Man United?
It doesn't matter which one
But it's about time someone did
And then they can be the new Premiership top gun.

So at the end of the season they sort out the score
Some fans cry, some fans smile
But all are left wishing for more
Unfortunately for them, they'll be waiting a while.

Robert Odey (15)
Bristol Grammar School

The Lounge Lizard

It's always there,
In front of the box,
Watching, watching,
Its eyes are locked.

While sun is shining,
Or during a blizzard,
Watching, watching,
Is the lounge lizard.

In pyjamas, slippers
And dressing gown,
Watching, watching,
Till after sundown.

While sun is shining,
Or during a blizzard,
Watching, watching,
Is the lounge lizard.

Anna Cheatle (16)
Bristol Grammar School

Some Random Haikus

A haiku is short
It's something you can be taught
But it needs some thought

A kitten is small
They like to play with a ball
They are really cool

School is a fun place
School dinners have a great taste
But I leave with haste

Fishing's really great
But you'll have to get some bait
And you'll need to wait.

Michael Bellew (14)
Bristol Grammar School

Dealing With The Hand You're Given

Dealing with ever-shuffling positions,
twelve majestic people,
in four different suits,
looking both ways,
and yet all two-faced.

Eight men holding weapons,
four women with flowers,
supported by their lower ranks,
four of whom have a greater power.

Black and red faces all through the pack,
fifty-two players make up this stack,
symbol of power led by a spade,
my heart will beat stronger,
than a diamond can shine,
membership to the club is of little value.

But all of them play whilst in this game.

Aaron Armoogum (15)
Bristol Grammar School

Revolution

The young man lies broken in the gutter
Passers look on, 'Capitalist,' they mutter

Peasants used to bow before him
Now all he has is the crap he lies on

Before all was needed was self-criticism
Now he's a scapegoat for Maoism

Mao rains terror at China's cost
Ideas supreme, no matter the loss.

Daniel Huggins (13)
Bristol Grammar School

Watcher

She went out of the house, walking along,
Unaware of surroundings, submerged in her song,
She never looked up at his painful stare,
Or to see him watching her, everywhere.

The sun was setting as she went down the high street
And saw her friends where they were due to meet.
They greeted each other the watcher still there,
But going unnoticed, without a care.

She returned up the high street at past midnight.
The road was in darkness with lack of streetlights.
She suddenly felt distinctly alone
And wanted so much to get back home.

Behind her some footsteps came to her ears
And into her eyes she felt present tears.
She started to run, heart pounding fast,
Finally she got to her house, at last.

She reached into her pocket and searched for the key,
She let herself in, after her, came he.

Victoria Ormerod (14)
Bristol Grammar School

Too Many Cooks

Clare put in thyme,
Zachary put in lime,
Joanna put in mango,
Oliver put in Tango,

Cecile whisked it,
Anna mixed it,
Sean folded it,
Eleanor scolded it,

Eugene dropped some,
Jenny scoffed some,
Amelia saved some,
Maxwell gave some,

Victoria ate the rest,
Then she was sick,
All down her vest,

Whilst wiping it up with a cloth,
She realised that,
Too many cooks do spoil that broth!

Alex Burrows (13)
Bristol Grammar School

Walking Along A Dusty Road

A man once lived
who walked and walked,
who walked along a road
this road, was long,
so long and straight
you could not see his goal
his goal, obscure
was to walk 40 days,
and 40 nights,
however long that is
he never reached the end
however because this road
was so long and straight
he slowed and slowed,
until he stopped,
then dropped,
in this sorry world.
No one knew,
this story was true,
about a man,
who walked and walked
for days and nights
that total 40 in all!

Andrew Miller (14)
Bristol Grammar School

God's Dogs

His eyes glazed over, as He stares at the wall,
He mumbles, 'Why'd I do it, why'd I do it at all?'

A wife and a husband alone at rest,
Maybe it was, maybe it was best.

My rain of tears, the wind of my hand,
The house could not take it, it could not stand.

Three days and four nights before they were found,
When they were found, got dragged to the pound.

Oh how they cried that night to go back home,
They could not stand it, being all alone.

Now God stares down from a gaping height
I shouldn't have done it, it wasn't right!

The kennel door rattled that night,
The dogs backed off, out of sight.

The bars bent and buckled, the dogs were free
They ran away back to home, they were free!

Then God looked up, He stares at the wall,
It turned out alright, alright after all.

Charlie Neale   (14)
Bristol Grammar School

Harabannanarbarbama

Three mongoosian steps over the milky moon,
You'll see a humble Barbumble tree
And in it should be a Margarababoon,
A roly-poly creature with eyes a-three
Picking out of the tree a harabannanarbarabama,
A fantastical, fantablible fruit
Covered in tongues which spit like a llama
Botanical, bomatical boots
With squirly heel and squimdidily toes
They may be quite quintessentially pretty
But be warned, if a bouncing boot should hit you on the nose,
You'll end up scrititty and bitty
In a garahtua of googleplex of precious pieces
So run, big-nosed children run, hurry and scurry
Three mongoosian steps over the moon, back to your mices,
Zoom, zoom, through shadow and gloom, home to
surreptitious Surrey.

Eleanor Seed (14)
Bristol Grammar School

My Brother Thinks

My brother thinks . . .
Food is for squashing and rubbing in your hair
Toy garages are for standing on to get everywhere;

Stairs are for climbing and falling down
Noses are for sticking fingers up to look like a clown;

Baskets of clothes are to go on the floor
A good thing about the kitchen is to open the door;

Crisp packets are crackly and make a good sound
Walking is hard so you fall on the ground;

Wipes are for sucking to get rid of the juice
But he's just a baby: that's his excuse!

Nikki Carver (11)
Colston's Girls' School

She Was Left Alone

The sun had gone,
There was nothing left but the girl.
Her hair was long and black like coal,
And her face was as white as a page.
She wandered the streets,
For hours and hours,
But she did not find her way.
She was lost in a world of darkness,
Where the air was blowing frost,
And she felt the chill.
She saw nothing, but heard everything,
The wind, the tears that slid down her face,
Her sobs, her sighs until,
Finally,
She was gone.

Sophie Fletcher (11)
Colston's Girls' School

Bonfire Night

Flames dancing, crackling
Red, yellow and amber,
Glowing in the angry red belly of the fire,
Licking up the wood and paper
I watch it crumple and turn to ash.

Fireworks
Bombs exploding in the sky
Raining down scarlet and gold
The 'oohs' and 'aahs' of the crowd,
As they watch the display above them.

In the morning nothing is left
But a pile of ash and a few glowing embers
The fire, disappearing slowly as memory fades
Until next year.

Jessica Coode (11)
Colston's Girls' School

Jamaica

Jamaica is bright
It's peaceful at night
You'll see wonderful waves
But very few caves
The sea is quite calm
It's the shape of your palm
There are trees to climb
There are juicy limes!

Jamaica is hot
It's as cosy as a cot
It's surrounded by the sea
It's the shape of a key
On the island there are mangoes
That taste like Tango!

Jamaica is cool
They don't have many rules
You'll definitely get a tan
So remember to bring a fan
You'll see lots of pretty flowers
As you sightsee through the hours.

Roxanne Osgood (10)
Colston's Girls' School

The Magical White Horse

He has a shiny coat of white
He is happiest at night
He has great power and might.

He has a silver mane
He likes to gallop on the plain
He has never worn a rein.

He always changes course
He has a mystical force
He is the magical white horse.

Verity Brant (11)
Colston's Girls' School

A Magic Pillow

I have a magic pillow
At night it sprouts two wings
It takes my thoughts away with it
And as it flies it sings:

'I am a magic pillow
At night I sprout two wings
I take your thoughts away with me
And as I fly I sing.'

When we get there, I climb off
And then we have a fight
This mighty pillow contest
Carries on each night.

Soon we have two pillows down
But the foe is closing in
Biff! Bash! Bosh! Three more are gone
There is an awful din.

It looks like we are winning
Ding! That's the final bell
I'll fight again tomorrow
But now, pillow fight, farewell!

Isabelle Denny (10)
Colston's Girls' School

Cornwall

Fill my lungs with this Cornish air!
As I dance and sing, people can stare.
Fill my heart with this Cornish love
As beautiful as the sky above.

Let me skip around the place
And shout and show my happy face.
Let me show the whole wide world,
For me its worth is more than gold!

Maisie Chilcott (11)
Colston's Girls' School

Autumn

Autumn has begun
Rustling trees
Children playing in the leaves
Do you think it's fun?

People are picking blackberries
And eating them raw,
Opening their mouths so wide
It's hurting their jaws.

The wind is blowing like a hurricane
Pushing people further and further away,
It's a good job they're wearing scarves and woolly hats
To keep the ferocious wind at bay.

Nights are getting darker,
Whilst Mars is getting brighter,
The trees are nearly bare
These are two signs of autumn
So you better beware.

Karimah Reid-Bailey (11)
Colston's Girls' School

My Big Sis

When my big sis smiles,
It's like a great big glow.
She really does show
When she's happy, when she's sad
And of course when she's mad.
She always brightens up my day
Whatever she may say.
She always rocks,
She always rolls.
When my big sis smiles,
It's like a great big glow.

Kirsty Bull (11)
Colston's Girls' School

Conker Trail

Down the garden path I go,
Knocking branches high and low,
I walk down the lane,
I see a key,
I see a bee,
Then I see a conker tree.

I pick up a branch,
'Ow!'
It's all prickly,
I pick up another,
I swing it high,
Right into the sky,
It lands in the tree,
Letting conkers fall right on to me,
I pick them up,
Put them in a cup,
I walk back up the lane,
Up the garden path,
Back through the door,
Slam!

Stephanie Stokes (11)
Colston's Girls' School

The Land Of The Young And Free

The land of the young and free,
That is where the soul of me
Strolls around, shows its face
In that dear familiar place.

Once we had a beautiful ground,
Now we've reduced it to a mound.
The Earth is in danger,
We've left it to strangers.
Why do people want to ruin this land?
Is it because they can?

Charlotte Lavin (11)
Colston's Girls' School

In 7K

In 7K there is . . .
Izzy with some geckos
Abi who loves red
Lisa who is lovely
And Zed who goes to bed
Marie is almost German
Steph does Irish dancing
Jess has tons of pets
And Sam who enjoys prancing
Lucy has a pony
Ali has a brother
Leyla speaks Turkish
And George's not like any other
Zanib has three sisters
Candace has a dog
Sarah has a rabbit
And Mary has a frog
Sophie has a brother
Zahra has two more
Hannah's been on holiday
And Megan's not a bore
Emily has a sister
Although Karimah has got two
Harry has a cousin
And Vicky has a rabbit
Last year it was new.

Mary Toth (11)
Colston's Girls' School

My Class 7K

Lucky Lucy she brings us good luck,
Miraculous Mary she knows when to duck,
Zigzag Zarah, she is keeping up a good pace,
Active Abi will win us the race,
Giggling George has the biggest of grins,
Sweet Sarah cheers up if we don't win,
Vampire Vicky she's not really that bad,
Happy Hannah, well I hope I'm not sad,
Killer Karimah, she keeps us in line,
Sassy Sam though stays out way past nine,
Sleeping Steph is dreaming of the best times,
I hope I'm not boring you with all these rhymes,
Zonking Zanib you'll never miss her,
Lovely Lisa's cat always wanting to purr,
Manic Megan she'll drive you up the wall,
Absolutely Alison, is she really that tall?
Irresistible Izzy has her head in the sky,
Zenith Zanib would never tell a lie,
Hyper Harry is bouncing up and down,
Energetic Emily is swarming round town,
Magnifique Marie is always the best
Super Sophie gives us a rest,
Jumping Jess is just a bunny
Crazy Candace is also rather funny
Loud Leyla would have microphones sacked
I've done everyone - and that's a *fact!*

Hannah Harrison (11)
Colston's Girls' School

Autumn

The leaves have left their owners now,
And are going to find some new ones
Now that autumn has come
There was absolutely no sign of the sun!

Foggy atmosphere ahead of me,
Crunchy, shrivelly leaves below me,
Snowflakes of leaves falling,
As if they were welcoming me!

With my gloves on my hands
And a scarf round my neck,
Out in the cold autumn wind,
I really, really wanted a peck!

I wished I could be home, by the warm fire,
I wished I could be home, having my tea,
The thoughts all made me homesick,
So I decided to rest under a tree!

On the way back home now,
My dream has at last come true,
I was feeling really cold,
So cold, I think I have the flu!

Safe and sound and warm now,
Sitting by the crackling fire,
Thinking of my autumn adventure,
Feeling the fire get higher and higher!

Zainab Wahid (11)
Colston's Girls' School

7K Crew

Sarah has a rabbit called Pongo,
George, two lizards, two dogs.
Izzy and Jess have lots of pets,
I wonder if they have frogs?

Emily's so loud, she's sure to cause a crowd,
Whilst Abbey's getting active,
Sam's trying to look attractive.
And Marie, she moved from Germany.

Mary has a cat called Maisy
Megan's just so mad, she's crazy
Leyla can speak Arabic and Turkish
And Steff does dancing that's Irish.

Harriet's cousin is going off to war
Hannah visited the Channel Islands to see the seashore.
Zed is extremely good at maths
And Candace likes nice long baths.

Zanib, Zarha and Alison all have brothers and sisters
Super Sophie works so hard, she has great big blisters.
And finally, but not the last
Lucy and Karimah who have been here in the past!

Who's the best?
7K, that's what I think anyway!

Megan Williams (11)
Colston's Girls' School

The 7K Poem

Zoinking Zed's just getting out of bed
As maniac Megan's thinking of something in her head
Zenith Zanib is on her way to the top,
Where as active Abbie's racing her to the spot.
Energetic Emily is thinking of something to do,
As sleepy Stephanie doesn't want anything new.
Killer Karimah will have you on the run,
When miraculous Mary just wants to have fun.
Lucky Lucy wants to play with pony Dave,
Whereas vampire Vicki's spying on her prey.
Hyper Harriet wants to jump around,
As sassy Sam's saving up for town.
Lovely Lisa just wants a laugh,
Whilst sweet Sarah's having a bath.
Irresistible Izzy is checking her looks,
When super Sophie flies in with some books.
Absolutely Alison just wants to mess around,
Whereas giggly George is nowhere to be found.
Happy Hannah just wants to go home,
Whereas loud Leyla's playing on her phone.

Marie Withers (11)
Colston's Girls' School

The Happy Horse

Her nostrils were wide,
Her head held high with pride.
She sailed over jumps,
She galloped over bumps,
Until she was free.

I did not see the flick of her tail,
No sign of her face so bay and pale.
I imagine her galloping with the herd,
But news of her, there's not been a word.

Ros McClelland (11)
Colston's Girls' School

The Hallowe'en Party

Jack-o'-lanterns on the trees
Singing in the chilly breeze
'Come to my party,' said the ghost,
'Eat and drink and burn the toast,
Have some smoked, juicy snails
Or a few roasted monkey tails,
Spider rolls and blood-bat wings,
Lizards fried and seaweed rings,
Choking venom, witches' brew
Or fizzy blood a sip or two.
Then let's play a mystery game,
Who's the victim?
Who's to blame?'
Cats are howling, witches groan
Skeletons playing on trombones
All night long, shiver and shake,
Eat frogs' legs and crispy snakes.

Alison Burbridge-Key (11)
Colston's Girls' School

Faces

The smile on your face reminds me of a banana
Although it might be a sultana.
The frown on your face reminds me of a lemon
Although it might be a clementine.
When you laugh
You should cut a peach in half.
When you cry
You should eat a dried apricot.
When you feel sad
You should look at a pineapple
Then you'll feel glad.
When you feel frightened, try to relax
Think of oranges, melons and tabby cats.

Lauren Jenkins (11)
Colston's Girls' School

My Classmates

Absolutely Alison says her brother's annoying,
Sleeping Steph says she does Irish dancing.
Lovely Lisa calls her cat Puppy,
Crazy Candace calls her dog Snowy.
Lucky Lucy's got a pony,
Magnifique Marie used to live in Germany.
While jumping Jessica's got a pet too many
Manic Megan's sister left this school.
Killer Karimah's trying to look cool
Energetic Emily's gazing at the bull.
Miraculous Mary's cat's playing with wool,
Zoinking Zanib's talking to herself as usual.
While loud Leyla's just being unusual.
Irresistible Izzy's showing off again
And vampire Vicky's doing the same.
Sassy Sam says she loves gym,
Happy Hannah's singing a hymn.
Giggly George calls one of her lizards Bruce Lee
And sweet Sarah's off to the sea.

Abioseh Harding (11)
Colston's Girls' School

Oh No!

I swirl dizzily
the world is closing in on me.
I try to breathe, in vain, I can't
shut out the witch's horrid chant
no fun, just terror now
like being butted in the back by a very large sow
trains roar, banshees scream
dinosaurs swoop, my mother's eyes gleam
she says, 'Get into bed Jo
you've got school tomorrow.'
Oh no!

Jessica Cooper (11)
Colston's Girls' School

The Black Cat

When I see the black cat at night,
I see his eyes first because they're so bright.
I then see the outline of his liquorice body
And then the tip of his tail.
I wonder if he can hear me,
If not, I know he can smell me.
I wish it was daytime because I could ruffle his fur.
But I think he would just jump over the wall.
He returns to my house every night
And bores his stony cold eyes into mine.
When the rain lands on his soft, coral nose,
He shivers, but ignores its wetness.
The rain knots his fur
And we know cats are vain.
He looks shocked at his appearance,
But I still think he looks beautiful.
So it really makes no difference
The black cat usually looks sleek and fine
Even in rain, he looks divine.

Emily Griffin (11)
Colston's Girls' School

Changing

The bright sun shines on the crisp autumn leaves,
Catching them as they fall from their branches,
Leaving behind the spring and summer
When they were bright and green and new.
Autumn takes us slowly and gently into winter,
When our landscape changes again
Into that fantasy season when white snowflakes fall
And children's excitement reaches fever-pitch.
Autumn brings us to the end of the year,
But also to new beginnings.

Katie Andrews (12)
Colston's Girls' School

Summer Fruit Salad

Summer fruits, summer fruits
Are juicy and fruity.

Fruity fruits, fruity fruits
Are crunchy and zesty.

Zesty fruits, zesty fruits
Are strawberry and berry.

Berry fruits, berry fruits
Are raspberry and cranberry.

Cranberry fruits, cranberry fruits
Are toothsome and squeezy.

Squeezy fruits, squeezy fruits
Are clementines and oranges.

Orange fruits, orange fruits
Are sour with citric acid.

Oh look! I've made my own summer fruit salad.

Hope Aikins (11)
Colston's Girls' School

My Brother

My brother is called Dwayne
He really is quite a pain
He likes the country Spain
And he also likes the rain
He really is annoying
And he keeps on snoring
He likes to play
But he never tidies away
He eats lots of chips
And he sails on many ships
I don't really like my brother
I wish I had another
One that *does not* bother.

Cecile Jones (11)
Colston's Girls' School

The Beach

The crystal-blue waves lash against the shore.
As I walk along the scorching sands
The fresh aroma of the salty sea air
Wisps at my face and breezes through my hair.
I can taste the brittle sand, gritty in my mouth
As my feet brush against the warm velvet sands
I hear children playing.

The sun beams down on me like a blinding ball of fire.
The sea glistens like diamonds in the sunlight,
The sand is like a desert stretching into the distance:
The beach is magical and somehow unreal, like an oasis.

The shells scattered about my feet are like corpses of a thousand lives.
As I paddle my feet in the sea
My toe brushes against the seaweed and sends a shiver up my spine
The familiar scent of fish tingles in my nose
And I hear the sea brush against the rocks.

Alice Daley (11)
Colston's Girls' School

The Big One

As I stepped towards the carriage, my tummy turned around,
I thought to myself, *It will be fine, just don't look down.*
I climbed into my seat and buckled up tight,
I looked up the track, it was of great height!
The horn sounded, we started to go,
The track was so steep, I preferred it low.
I smelt my own fear, getting to the top
And even more when it started to drop!
I heard the deafening screams from in front and behind,
It was whizzing so fast, I almost lost my mind!
It whirled and twirled then came to a stop,
With my eyes closed tight, I thought it would drop.
But then I heard others getting off,
What a wonderful roller coaster ride that was!

Katie Dilleigh (11)
Colston's Girls' School

Autumn

Late September with the wind and rain,
The leaves start to fall again and again,
The wind blows them around
Until they hit the cold, icy ground
Carpets of leaves cover the grass
Making a long thick cast.

Late October the trees are bare
Like they have no bushy green hair
Standing tall and dark
In the cold, lonely park.

Late November comes red and gold,
Browns and scarlets, colours bold,
Lying on the covered ground
Always making a crispy sound,
But soon they will get covered in frost
Snow will be there and leaves will be lost.

Sarah Mowling (11)
Colston's Girls' School

A Few Of My Favourite Things

Pretty pink petals and bright butterflies
Chocolate ice cream and my cat's sparkly eyes
The smell of wet grass when you've just woken up
Breakfast in bed and warmth in a cup
Acting in plays and having to sing
These are a few of my favourite things

Cute little babies and small tiny creatures
Friends who are loyal and wonderful teachers
Waking up on weekends then back to bed
Quiet nights in or ones out instead
Colourful parrots with feathery wings
These are a few of my favourite things.

Charlotte Coupland (11)
Colston's Girls' School

Bristol

Bristol is a rainy place,
It hasn't got a lot of space,
All that's in it is lots of cars,
I wish I could zoom off straight to Mars;
Bristol is a rainy place.

Bristol is a rainy place,
People walk at a very quick pace,
It's full of lots of lousy litter,
It's very cold and very bitter;
Bristol is a rainy place.

Bristol is a rainy place,
You never find a happy face,
The air is full of putrid pollution,
You can never find a good solution
For no one wants to live in Bristol;
Bristol is a rainy place!

Lucy Rudge (11)
Colston's Girls' School

Television

Have you ever been told by Mum or Dad
If you sit too near the telly then you may go mad?
Now let me please tell you that they are truly right
Next time you watch it you may get an awful fright
Your eyes for certain are bound to go square
And if you're not careful your mind will go bare
If you go to the doctor's to find a cure
There is not one and that's for sure
So please do be careful not to get this disease
I'll bow down on my hands and knees
For you to stay away from this wretched TV
Take these points and that's all from me.

Jocelyn Head (11)
Colston's Girls' School

Cat At The Window

There's a cat at my window
But I can't get to it.
There's a cat at my window
But I can't get out.
There's a cat at my window
I'd love to play, but if I opened the window
It'd run away.
I feel really jealous as
The cat is staring at me,
But I don't stare back.
I walk outside,
But it ignores me.
Now if I were a cat
And the cat was me,
I'd want a treat
And it would want to play with me.
There's a cat at my window
I get a toy mouse,
There's a cat at my window
But it just stares in the house.
There's a cat at my window
But look over there
Another cat!
But I'd love to play with the one on the sill
There's a cat at my window
I know, I'll make the cat jealous
And give this other cat the treats!
There was a cat at my window
But now it's playing with me,
I love the cat and it loves me!

Catherine Stewart (11)
Colston's Girls' School

Just One More Stitch

An inheritance from a great-aunt
She never met,
A mere one thousand dollars
To add to the rest.
Just one more stitch in the perfect silk blanket
Covering her, protecting her,
And making sure that
She'll never have to work,
That's in America.
Another football, made painstakingly,
Stitch by stitch, after two weeks of toil,
Under poor light, and in bad conditions.
Every tiny stitch through the rough leather matters,
Just one more stitch, then one more,
May be just enough for her
To survive for one more day,
That's in Africa.
Here you have the lives of two girls, both fourteen:
One with the world at her feet
And the other so far under it
That she hasn't reached Australia yet.
One for whom normal is
Shopping in designer boutiques;
The other has never done anything
But stitch after tedious stitch.
Two human beings:
One sews her own story,
The other is sewn into hers;
One with rights; one without,
In the same world . . . why?

Isobel Booth (13)
Colston's Girls' School

The Grey Horse

The boy paused and said,
'What do you see?'
'I've seen the ghosts of horses three.'
The young boy stood awhile in thought
His forehead creased, the answer he sought.
'The black is for truth,
The white is deceiving,
The grey is lost,
In mourning, grieving.'
'Then sister,' he said, 'the grey is mine
White is yours, you are dead, just in my mind.'
'I am not dead!' the young girl cried
The boy shook his head, and quietly sighed
But before he could speak the girl faded away,
The tears poured down, in silent dismay.
'The black belongs to war and peace
The truth comes out when nothing sleeps.'

Amelia Tennant (11)
Colston's Girls' School

The Poem

This poem is neither short nor long
It's not a story nor a song.
It's got seven words in each line
And in them they each have a rhyme.

It's twelve lines as you can see
The author of the poem is me!
It's got no meaning, it's just words
It is most strange and quite absurd!

Each line starts with a capital letter
You should read it, you'll feel better
To this poem I found an end
Before I went right round the bend!

Becky Lawrence (11)
Colston's Girls' School

At The Seaside

There's sand in my hair
And sand on my nose.
There's sand in my eyes
And sand between my toes.

There's sand in my sandwiches
And sand in my tea.
There's sand in my cake
And sand on my knee.

There's sand in my hat
And sand in my shoe.
There's sand in my sock
Where my toe pokes through.

It's time to go home now.
The day's almost done,
But we're coming back tomorrow,
To enjoy loads more fun.

Michele George (12)
Colston's Girls' School

A Winter's Tale

Ice was forming on the pond,
The cold water crystals forming a bond,
Ice skaters skating across the frozen lake,
Patterns of circles and lines they make.

Children making snowmen
Using old winter clothes,
Coal for his eyes and a carrot for his nose.

Sledges sliding down snowy hills,
Giving their riders lots of thrills,
Parents watching their children play,
Children saying they could play all day.

Amelia Northcott (11)
Colston's Girls' School

Leaping Dolphins

Down by our tent, we were mucking about,
Jim came running calling us.
'Come to the beach quickly,' he urged.
'Dolphins are jumping, do come and see.'
Down on the beach, people were hushed,
Pointing and peering out to sea.
So we sat in a row, looking quite hard.
Then we saw one, no two or maybe it's three?
Cruising towards us closer and closer they came,
Till they stopped by the rocks and swam back out to sea.
As they swam away they began jumping and playing,
Arching their bodies as they leapt out of the sea
Leaping and playing into the distance,
Further and further away they went
Until waves and dolphins looked the same.
We watched the sea long after they'd gone,
Sitting on the beach sea breeze in our hair,
Watching the sun setting over the bay.
Golden and red, shimmering on the sea.

Isabelle Peters (11)
Colston's Girls' School

Mama The Beauty Queen

'Beauty is the best'
That's what my mama said
Putting on her mascara
On her fine feather eyelash.
She's beautiful like a swan
With her long black wavy hair
And her luscious lips like cherries
And her cheeks are rouged like strawberries.
She fills my heart with joy
And sometimes she buys me toys.
Mama always says
Beauty is the best.

Lavana Brown (12)
Colston's Girls' School

Horror Film

As I sit, my head buried
Deep into the cushion,
I dare to turn
But as I turn, I see
There is no eye,
Just a red, empty socket,
Where one trail of blood oozes out.
I scream.
Terrified I scream.
To the safety of the cushion I turn, when
Suddenly
There is another electrifying scream,
But this time it's not mine.
A grip tightens onto me
And my heart stops.
What happened?
What happened after that eye?

Agnes Davidson (12)
Colston's Girls' School

Garden Bound

The beaming sun promptly arrives,
Its scorching rays push me inside.
I think I'll go for a refreshing sleep,
But as dreams tumble off I'm unwilling to peek.
My head pokes out, nippy as a kangaroo,
I take a swift gripping glance or two.
The multicoloured bundle of the sun has gone,
So here's my chance but not for long.
I have a cool well-earned drink,
But soon it's time to slowly sink.
Back I slide into my homely shell,
Do you know my secret?
Well please don't tell
That I'm just a lonely little garden snail.

Aimeé-Claire Eyermann (12)
Colston's Girls' School

Worst Things

My sister, a drag,
She makes me feel bad,
The way we sit at the table,
I hate doing the stable,
Car light bright,
Noises in the night,
Mushy peas,
Bumblebees,
Rubbish on the floor,
A knock at the door,
Rats and mice,
Itchy headlice,
The people at the bank,
The water in a tank,
The bite of a shark,
The pitch-black dark,
Leftover food,
The way I'm in a mood,
Last year's band,
Playing in the sand,
Afraid of heights,
I don't like a fright,
Goodbye I say,
Until another day!

Polly Tucker (12)
Colston's Girls' School

Cats

C arefully creeping
A dventurously ambling
T errifying, teasing
S wiftly stalking shadows.

Eleanor Longhurst (12)
Colston's Girls' School

Night

Night like a burglar gets ready to steal and scare,
His face is as black as a panther.
His long ebony cloak floats over the world.
The moon opens, the stars blink,
He comes around at bedtime.

He loves to eat Milky Ways and galaxies,
The other stars are the piercing of his body.
He's ready to roam and wander about,
His tall jet-black hat puts wicked things into sleepy heads.

You can hear him bellowing to the planets,
The sun is his enemy.
Night blinds you and turns the world black,
His home is in the clouds.

Carla Sims (12)
Colston's Girls' School

The Black Night

It's a dark, dark night
A black cat purrs
Turns around shouts, 'Miaow'
And gives a fright.

The street lights glow
Like the shining sun
The cars go by cautiously
Like a tortoise, and as slow.

The wind blows on the black cat's fur
The black cat creeps on
It purrs and purrs
The streetlights turn off
And the black night is silent.

Sunia Malik (12)
Colston's Girls' School

I'm Scared

I'm scared of a shark,
I'm scared of the dark,
I'm scared of a snake,
But not of daybreak.

I'm scared of rats,
I'm scared of bats,
I'm scared of dogs,
But not of frogs.

I'm scared of bullies calling me names,
I'm scared of angry fire flames,
I'm really scared of growing up,
But not of a friendly coffee cup.

I'm scared of attackers having a kick,
I'm scared of people taking the mick,
I'm scared of everything that's new,
But I have to say I'm not scared of *you!*

Polly-RuAnna Martin (12)
Colston's Girls' School

Chocolate

Rustling, rustling the wrapper tears.
Rustling, rustling too good to share.
Chocolate, chocolate melting on your tongue,
Chocolate, chocolate now it's all gone.
Yum, yum it's dark and rum.
Yum, yum as I lick my thumb.
Tummy, tummy gurgling inside;
Tummy, tummy all satisfied!

Jasmine Richards-Marsh (12)
Colston's Girls' School

A Walk In Autumn

Snap, crackle, pop as our feet step down,
Treading on a rainbow of leaves scattering all around.
Golden syrup-yellow leaves dancing in the sun,
Run to catch the leaves, I can't catch one!
Sweet, juicy berries hiding among the thorns,
Taste as good as Heaven, fresh, new and warm.
Conkers all around us weighing down the trees,
Smooth and soft and rounded, perfect in every way.
Walking past a bonfire, red and golden shine,
As bright as sunlight and look there's Guy!
People with sparklers like a magic wand,
Harry Potter would be jealous they're better than his one!
The fireworks are a light soaring into the air,
Then swirling round and staying still until the sky is bare
People cheer and ask for more, we carry on walking.
Until we reach our warm, welcoming home,
Where we snuggle up in bed with a warm cocoa.

Eleanor Head (12)
Colston's Girls' School

The Living Dead

Creepy winds howl with delight
Hallowe'en has come so prepare for a fright!
Smoky atmosphere makes the mood
Corpses and zombies will arrive soon.
Beware of those vampires they will creep out,
Werewolves and witches will rise no doubt
Staircases creeping
Footsteps on the floor
Bangs and knocks break down your door!
Ghostly sounds enter your room,
Before you know it you've met your doom . . .

Aliah Malik (12)
Colston's Girls' School

Different

They jeer, they sneer,
I fight better than them.
They gasp, trying to mask
The fact that I ride like the men.
I fence, I have sense.
When I rebel they say I smell.
'Witch! Bitch!'
Their hateful chant.
'Be a lady!'
'No, I can't!'
Why can't they see who I really am?
Why can't I be me?
I am locked in a cage,
They have thrown away the key,
Just because I am different.

Natasha Filer (12)
Colston's Girls' School

What I Wanted

I am different
I know I am.
They wanted me
To prance on a pony
But I wanted to fence.
They wanted my hair
Scrunched up in a little bun,
But I wanted it long and flowing.
They wanted me to be
Quiet and polite
But I wanted to shout out to the whole world.
They wanted me
To get perfect grades
But I'm most familiar with Fs
They wanted me to fit in -
But I can't.

Abra Thompson (12)
Colston's Girls' School

Autumn Days

Big fat conkers lying on the ground,
Leaves falling off trees.
You can tell it's autumn
By the smell.

Children jumping in piles of leaves
Collecting too.
Children really like autumn
There are lots of things to do.

Blackberries are ripe
So people can pick
And make yummy treats,
Like blackberry pie.

Autumn is nearly over,
What am I going to do?
Autumn is nearly over,
What am I going to do?

Emma Willding (12)
Colston's Girls' School

Winter

Every house covered in a white blanket,
Water as hard as stone,
Snowflakes as delicate as china,
One child all on her own.

Cold winter nights,
Cold winter mornings,
Cold winter afternoons,
Cold winter evenings.

The only colours are red and green,
Christmas trees in every house,
No living leaf can be seen,
This is what I like about *winter.*

Elizabeth Copeland (12)
Colston's Girls' School

The Spotted Army

We watched in silence
As our army fell,
Crashing to the ground.
We watched in silence
As our army fell,
Tumbling all around.

We watched in silence
As the soldiers brave
Closed their weary eyes.
We watched in silence
As the soldiers brave
Lay still beneath the skies.

In that army of black,
Who was the first . . .
To start the fall;
The trip;
The stumble;
The stagger;
The swoon?

We watched in silence;
White spots on black uniforms
Winked at a failing sun.

Daisy Woods (12)
Colston's Girls' School

The Five Senses Of Autumn

The smell of the cool autumn air.
The feel of the glossy conkers freshly picked of the conker tree.
The look of the crisp, crimson leaves.
The gorgeous taste of the recently picked apples from
An apple tree at the bottom of your garden.
And the sound of happy children playing in the crackling leaves.

April Miller (12)
Colston's Girls' School

My Friend!

It's so nice to have a friend
Someone you can rely on
Someone who is always
With a shoulder to cry on

A friend will always be there
Whenever you need to talk
You'll always have her good advice
She will lead the way to walk

A friend is someone caring
Who will never lead you astray
When you're feeling down or blue
She'll help you all the way

So never take your friend for granted
You know you'll always need her
Always trust her, let her know
That you really need to keep her.

Catherine Ann Manaei (12)
Colston's Girls' School

Attack!

I'm walking under the bridge
When I hear footsteps behind me.
Getting closer and closer.
I look around but there's nobody there.
As I carry on walking, in the distance
I see someone walking towards me.
I start to panic and I walk faster
My heartbeat gets heavier.
Soon I know something is going to happen and
Just as I get to the corner of my street
My assailant confronts me.
Ambushed, I scream in despair then to my surprise from behind,
My guardian angel rushes to my rescue.

Khadijah Murchison (12)
Colston's Girls' School

Apples In Autumn Time

Crunchy, crispy apples,
Falling to the ground,
Those sweet and juicy apples,
Just waiting to be found.

Sitting amongst a bed of leaves,
But they are all bright,
With scarlet glistening apples,
Sparkling through the night.

The apples are glossy splodges,
Some of them are lime,
Lying there so beautifully,
That's what you get in autumn time.

Crimson, maroon and moss,
Russet, yellow and green,
They are lovely colours,
More lovely than I've ever seen.

Samantha Parker (12)
Colston's Girls' School

My Cat!

I lift the 13-week-old kitten from his mum.
He stretches like a tree bending softly in the wind.
Sits on my hand like a leaf on the ground
And looks at me all quiet and scared.
Two little brown eyes like shiny conkers,
He miaows like a door opening,
Curls up like a hedgehog (scared)
He comes home miaowing like a wolf,
Wondering where he is;
Home at last!

Hannah Mogford (12)
Colston's Girls' School

Autumn

Autumn leaves are falling,
Falling everywhere.
The scrunching and crunching
The leaves are a crisp crimson colour
I love to go for a walk,
To see the conkers falling,
The conkers fall like hedgehogs.

Autumn is the time of year
When the hot weather fades away
People wrap up in lots of clothes.

Then it's November
With the whizzing and banging.
I love to watch the fireworks:
I enjoy seeing the showering colour
And the smell of hot soup
It drips down your throat.

End of autumn is drawing near,
We will have to wait another year.
Never mind, winter is just as good,
Especially with all the food.

Laura Maggs (12)
Colston's Girls' School

The One And Only!

It's 12 o'clock! The clock has struck!
Time for the one and only!
Shall I open my eyes and take a peek,
Or keep them closed and go to sleep?

As church bells peal, I stir and wake,
My eyes wide open for Christmas Day
And I see that again, I have missed my dream,
To see the one and only.

Rachael Irving (12)
Colston's Girls' School

The Beach

The sand is welcomed by my toes,
As I walk along the beach.
I watch as the sun slowly goes,
Beneath the waves to sleep.

The rocks await my presence,
As I start towards the cliffs.
I leap and climb to the top of them,
With the sea's salty kiss.

I reach the top and sit there,
Gasping air for a while.
Then I leap and climb two steps at a time,
To the water's familiar chill.

The day is done I know now,
As the night is embracing the beach.
It's time to sleep, rest my eyes and feet,
As a new day is in my reach.

Laura Curry (12)
Colston's Girls' School

Bored

My eyes are sore
From facing the wall.
Tick-tock:
That's the clock.
Bare feet,
Cars beep.
Drip drop,
Close the tap.
Tummy rumbles,
Funny grumbles.
Wind gushes,
Mum rushes.
Dad snores,
Life's a bore.

May Kay Ho (12)
Colston's Girls' School

Why Does No One Like Me?

Why does no one like me?
Just because I am different,
Just because I have glasses,
Does not make me different.
Why does no one like me?
Just because I am different,
Just because I have black shiny hair,
Does not make me different.
Why does no one like me?
Just because I am different,
Just because I wear black clothes,
Does not make me different.
Why does no one like me?
Just because I am different,
Just because I have piercing,
Does not make me different.
Why does no one like me?
Just because I am different
Just because I listen to weird music . . .
OK maybe it does make me different.

Alice Saunders (12)
Colston's Girls' School

The Winter Magpie

The snowflakes whirl and twirl around me,
Gentle crunching beneath my feet,
Silence fills the glistening street,
Trees swaying in the morning light,
I catch a glint of something bright,
A magpie holding a special ring,
It drops it suddenly and starts to sing,
Away, away it flies,
Leaving me with this perfect prize.

Ariana Ahmadi (12)
Colston's Girls' School

The Wood!

In the wood when spring is near
The animals come out and sniff the air
For any hunter that might be near
The ground gets warm
The buds come out
All the squirrels scuffle about,
For there's hoards which they packed last year,
Nuts galore!

As dusk approaches on this first night
When the ground gets warm
The buds come out
The hedgehogs, badgers and foxes appear
Prowling the ground for anything near
Cause they are hungry with nothing about for two months!
Some will hibernate
How clever are they!
But, foxes prowl all the year round.

As summer approaches near the end of spring
This time of year
The lambs are born in the fields of sheep
And in the wood the birds are twittering
Diving about, while their chicks are cheeping
Waiting for food
Soon the solemn stag approaches with is graceful does
Then the frisky fawns wander
Unaware of the dangers around them.

As autumn comes
The birds fly their nests
The fawns now know the dangers around them
Nothing can see them, they disappear into a shower of leaves
Red, gold and brown they fall to the ground
When you step on them they crunch
The animals are preparing for winter
Collecting the nuts, some are preparing for hibernation

The winter is approaching
Soon all is quiet
The animals are going into their nests
It is getting quieter and quieter
The snow starts to fall then it settles
Now it is silent.

Sophie Dennis (12)
Colston's Girls' School

Autumn Leaves

Down, down, down
Fall the golden drops of autumn,
Trampled and torn.

Crackle, crunch, squish, scrunch
As they leave the world they know so well,
Trampled and torn.

They gracefully fly through the air,
Like ballerinas drifting
Through the dark, cold night.

How can they cope?
How can they stay
At the bottom, where they are so far away
From the place they used to know?

How can they sleep?
How can they keep
Such beautiful colours when
All they do is lie there?

Crackle, crunch, squish, scrunch
As they slowly drift away.

Christiana Tziorta (13)
Colston's Girls' School

Night Of Day

The moon was a golden galleon
Being tossed upon cloudy shores
The stars were like butterflies
Fluttering through cloudy moonlit doors
Stop . . . a breath of silence

A gush of wind came riding
Riding, riding
A storm of rain came riding
From the empty Earth below

Crash, bang, a flash of light!
Now all is clear

The sky was a clear blue lake
The sun a radiant beam
White clouds would bow
At this amazing scene.

Stop, a breath . . . of silence . . .

Breannah-Marie Sawyers (12)
Colston's Girls' School

Baby Tears

I started to cry as I dropped my dummy,
Turned around couldn't find Mummy.

Tall, large people looked my way,
Stared and talked saying wait and stay.

Speakerphone message for my mum,
I saw her then, I started to run.

She picked me up and twirled me round,
Then put me back upon the ground.

She kissed me and called me her little dear,
Then wiped away my baby tears.

Nicola Martin (13)
Colston's Girls' School

The Shipwreck

The splashing of the deep blue sea,
The ticking of the sea-faring clock,
Tick-tock, tick-tock.

The noise of the swirling waves,
The slapping as the wind hits the sails,
The struggle to steer a course.

The ticking of the sea-faring clock,
Tick-tock, tick-tock.

The crashing of the boat hitting the water,
The clicking and clattering
As the pans scatter around.

The ticking of the sea-faring clock,
Tick-tock, tick-tock.

The flash of lightning, the crack of thunder,
The explosion of the hull on the rocks,
Tick-tock, tick-tock,
The shipwreck lapping on the seashore.

Tick-tock, tick.

Ali Clark (13)
Colston's Girls' School

Tropical Isle

The sun is as hot as a furnace, well heated for the game.
See how it gleams off the pure zinc.
The sun scorches the life out of the simmering golden sands,
But people of this land rely on its rays,
As their source of heat and light.

The sea is an ocean of crystal clear ice.
Its great blue waves usher in the foaming tide,
As milk being fed to a baby,
Coconut husks dance on the salty sea like little brown boats,
While the people of this land buzz back and forth, so busy.

Monique Henderson (12)
Colston's Girls' School

I Am Opening My Drawer

I am opening my drawer,
What's there?
A white dress is there,
It has frilly sides
It's been there for years.
It's my special christening dress.

I am opening my drawer
What's there?
A brown bear is there
Soft, small and lying there.

I am opening my drawer
What's there?
My hat which I wore
When my sister was a bridesmaid
It's straw and blue.

I am opening my drawer
What's there?
My rocking sheep is there
My first Christmas sheep was there,
It's white and fluffy, soft too.

I am opening my drawer
What's there?
A photo of my first bike,
Pink and white.
I closed my drawer but my memories are still there.

Chloe Green (12)
Colston's Girls' School

In My Cupboard

In my cupboard,
There is a teddy bear,
It has brown fur
And big black eyes.

In my cupboard,
There is a silver dress,
Covered in tiny hearts and circles
It was my very first birthday gift.

In my cupboard,
There is a photo album,
It is a rectangle covered in glitter,
It brings me back the memories from the past.

In my cupboard,
There is a black leathery shoe,
It is tiny but very old and dirty,
I wore it when I had little feet.

In my cupboard,
There is a bike,
Old and rusty,
My very first bike.

So this is a poem,
When I was little,
It brings me the memories.

Priyanga Sarma (12)
Colston's Girls' School

I Would Love To Travel The World

I would love to travel the world
And help every poor country.
I would love to help every child
In having the childhood they deserve.
I would love to stop terrorism,
It makes everyone so upset and mad.
I would love to help every country
Join hands and make peace.
I would love every religion and race
To respect each other and join as one.
I would love every harmful weapon
To be banned and destroyed.
I would love every person
To be able to sleep at night, knowing they are safe.

But I cannot be so ambitious
When my home country is far from perfect.

Yasmin Dalton (14)
Colston's Girls' School

The Joy Of Autumn

The third season rose upon a dull winter,
A time for the conkers to appear,
Starting off as green shells,
As spiky as hedgehogs.
Then the auburn ones are here.
It's time for fun and games galore.
From early till late, crimson leaves will fall.

Conical clusters are everywhere,
The smell of vinegar is in the air,
Conker competitions are all around,
Their smashing can be heard,
Happiness is also there.

Winter is now here,
But the joy of autumn will always be near.

Becky Evans (12)
Colston's Girls' School

A Very Tense Moment

There she goes on her small white toes,
She's doing well at the moment,
I hope she wins this ballet thing
And returns with a gold medal home.

She is competing with many other ballerinas,
Her hair up in a bun and her make-up seems
Transparent except for her lips that shine in the sun.

Many people are watching my girl
Do classical on stage and people clap
When she does something well.

There she goes on her small white toes,
She's nearly there, just a few more steps
Will do the trick and she holds as solid as
A brick on one toe aching for her balance.
Two, three, four and she's done it,
Congratulations!

Mariam Afzal (13)
Colston's Girls' School

Imagine What It Is Like In Heaven

Imagine what it is like in Heaven.
A big golden gate as you enter,
Angels greeting you.

Imagine what it is like in Heaven.
There's no way out,
But there is no reason to escape.

Imagine what it is like in Heaven.
Looking down on Earth,
Maybe watching people live their life, dream their dream.

Imagine what it is like in Heaven.
Is there a Heaven?

Sian Basham (12)
Colston's Girls' School

Fleeing

As two leaders decide their country's fate, a family flees,
The leaders, they just can't agree,
Knowing that soon there will be planes overhead,
The family do not want to be among the dead.

A man hiding from the law,
The public scared as they hear what he did before,
People begged to keep calm,
Terrified that they may come to some harm.

A fox separated from its family, attempts to run
From the hounds and hunters who kill foxes for fun,
The poor creature's cornered and it shuts its eyes,
The hunters' laugh as the young fox prepares to die.

A young girl sitting on the streets, watches passers by day,
They are passing but in the same spot she stays,
Instead of a suitcase she has bruises from her mum and dad,
Since she can remember she has been a human punch bag.

They push him and shove him to the ground,
He gets up and stumbles around,
The ten-year-old boy spots a shop, it's not too far,
Runs into the road and into the path of an oncoming car.

Anna Wardell (13)
Colston's Girls' School

The Lonesome Flower

The lonesome flower danced in the autumn breeze,
Among the dead grass it looked like fireworks in a midnight sky,
The flower was beautiful, bright colours like a roaring fire.
The lonesome flower danced and danced in the farmer's field,
A strong breeze shocked the flower
And plucked the petals off one by one.
The lonesome flower danced naked in the farmer's field,
Not so beautiful anymore;
Its beauty lost forever.

Chantelle Dowe (12)
Colston's Girls' School

The Wife's Revenge

See here's the grave
Of my darling wife,
She was very trusty too;
But she should have
Never trusted me
'Cause I never followed through.

Now today I am still alive,
I wish she was here too;
Then I could erase
What I did;
Then I could stop living with
The guilt, each day through
And through.

I know she did not betray me,
I should have known then,
I cannot live with this
Over my head,
So I am thrusting myself
Into *Hell's* end.

Zuwena Reid-Bailey (13)
Colston's Girls' School

The Whale

His long, agile body
Swiftly and silently travels through the still, calm water,
Singing and sharing his sweet lullaby.
Up, up he goes with all his strength
Then *splash!*
Soon he brings himself down, still
Singing his sweet lullaby.
Eventually he moves away, tired,
Ready for a new adventure,
Looking for more in the deep, dark ocean.

Rachel Jackson (12)
Colston's Girls' School

Secrets Kill

As she wept upon the grave, her sodden napkin in her hand
If only she had told him about her love for a young man.

Her age of only sweet sixteen, her father at his death
She did not tell her dad about the handsome boy she met.

A boy of eighteen, from a village
Had just asked her hand in marriage.

She was not sure about the wedding
She lay sprawled across her satin bedding.

Did she love him or love being loved?
She prayed to her father in the sky above.

'Father I have deceived you. I hope you can forgive
I am to be wed, though you may not know who with.'

'How much I long to be there, be united with you
Right now I do not know what on earth I am going to do.'

She then pulled out a knife sharp enough to split a hair
She decided what to do as she stood up, then and there.

She lurched over to her balcony, mounted the cold stone railing
Knife in hand, tears streaming, wailing.

'Father forgive me,' she called, overwhelmed with emotions
She slit her throat with one smooth motion.

Eyes grey, cheeks pale,
Body weakened, cold and frail.

She collapsed and fell, out of sight
Through the icy mist of the November's night.

Camelia Chowdhury (13)
Colston's Girls' School

Life In Motion

The Pacific Ocean is life in motion beneath the tidal waves
Marine life dive to stay alive as they dart into shallow caves.

They all have a name in my little game as I christen every one
Now I'll tell you a story it's a world of glory as they dance
                                                    beneath the sun.

Colin the crab was looking quite drab as he sat on the cold sea floor
Half buried in sand and oh so grand as he moved his razor-
                                                    sharp claw.

Just above and so in love Miriam the mermaid girl
With her golden hair and a look so rare she tumbled and did a swirl.

Stan the shark was having a lark as he displayed his razor-sharp teeth
As he looked for his prey he decided to stay among the coral reef.

Along came Kay the manta ray, so graceful and serene
Gliding and sliding, no reason for hiding, I wonder where she's been.

Wally the whale splashed his tail as he rose above the surf
The seabed rumbled and large rocks tumbled as he displayed
                                                    his giant girth.

An ugly fish shaped like a dish swam with a half-eaten fin
As the bubbles came out of his bulbous snout they battered
                                                    his scaly skin.

A dolphin called Don swam along with his family by his side
A school of fish swooshed and swished then jumped on for a ride.

As the plant life sways the sealife plays without a care or thought
The tide cannot hide this magical world in which my imagination
                                                    is caught.

Alexandra Hucker (13)
Colston's Girls' School

A Starry Night At Sea

The stars hung in the midnight sky, shining bright,
Casting a silver glow on the streets of London,
The city was sprinkled with jewels of light,
And swallows swam through the darkness of the night.

A million miles away, a girl lay in a boat,
In the turquoise soothing sea, just afloat,
The sand was as white as snow,
And the water clear as glass, below.

Then the waves grew outrageous and wild,
And grey crystals fell from up above,
The raindrops woke the sleeping child,
Overhead, black storm clouds piled.

Far-off, a ship's bell could be heard,
Noisy as a frantic bird,
Her alarm was ringing, she realised,
She sat up in bed and opened her eyes.

Beth Brown (13)
Colston's Girls' School

Smile

No one knew as she walked away,
With the knife so clearly near,
That she was to be alone,
As the act made her disappear.

She found an alley, dank and dreary,
To get rid of the sin within,
To slide the blade, poor fearful maid
And see what death will bring.

Then found alone, in a pool of blood,
Their hearts began to race,
As they saw this girl on the floor,
With a smile upon her face.

Ngaio Anyia (13)
Colston's Girls' School

Life Is All About Motion!

Life is all about motion,
The birds and the bees,
The cats and the fleas,
Eating, drinking,
Talking, thinking,
Life is all about motion.

Life is all about motion,
Running, talking,
Singing, dancing,
Laughing, prancing,
Life is all about motion.

Life is all about motion,
The athletes run,
The flowers sway,
We eat and drink,
We run and play,
Life is all about motion.

Keely Shepherd (13)
Colston's Girls' School

Racism

It's eating people's insides,
Chased by screams and sniggers.
The pain is choking,
Suffocating all thoughts,
A wounding to the soul,
Echoing around fresh scars,
Blowing fuses, causing stabbing.
They don't mean it! They do!
Stabbing me, shocking me, killing me:
The harsh words that only true hatred can spit,
The sick words, the sick words of *racism*.

Hannah Ricketts (13)
Colston's Girls' School

The Thrill Of The Hunt

The church clock struck twelve. This was her cue.
Softly, silently, her silken paws led her out into the night,
Leaving the stuffy air of the barn behind.
The clouds were floating across the heavens,
Hiding the moon from view.
This was the sensation she lived for; the reason she had been born.
Her feline body mingled with the darkness, and they became one.
As she moved through the dark alleyways,
Her sensitive nose catching scents from every direction,
Her anticipation grew and grew.
Her slim body, her proud posture and her delicate senses
Made her feel at one with the world.
As she neared her hunting grounds for the night
Her acute senses picked up everything around her.
Her ears heard the pattering of minute feet,
Her nose picked up the smell of a young rat.
She followed her prey, stalking it silently.
Her unknown victim led her into a nearby graveyard
Where it scuttled over the eroding graves.
She froze, still as a rock. Her muscles tensed -
Suddenly she sprang.
She landed softly on her padded paws, picking up her prey.
Enveloped in darkness she slunk back into the open streets,
Leaping onto a high brick wall to devour her meal in peace.

Hannah Hare (13)
Colston's Girls' School

Water

W is for water that fills the ocean wide.
A is for atlas that shows where it lies.
T is for tears that wet our dry faces.
E is for eels which roam the ocean places.
R is for rain that drip, drops down the windowpane.

Anastasia Smith (13)
Colston's Girls' School

Looks

What are looks exactly?
Are they a way to judge?
If we all looked the same,
Would people hold a grudge?
So what if you wear glasses,
Does it mean that you are smart?
So what if you have blonde hair,
Does it mean that you're a tart?
You may not be good-looking,
What about personality?
And I know there isn't a law
Against originality,
We don't know why God gave us looks,
There's nothing in the holy books.
But if you do not give a damn,
Then everyone'll be your fan.

Sophie O'Kelly (13)
Colston's Girls' School

The Silent Song Of The Stream

The trickle and a-dribble as the stream flows on,
And the swaying of the trees in the warm morning sun,
The stream faster now, picking up rocks and stones,
Twirling, spinning, swishing, swashing as the wind begins to moan,
Trees shake, thunder breaks, but the storm is just beginning.
The stream grows wider, crashing, bashing, swirling, twirling, clinging,
The wind is howling like a dog, it's prowling, growling, baring its teeth,
Trees are upturned but the river flows on like a drumbeat from beneath,
Suddenly, a silence, nothing moves and the trees are still,
From beneath a cloud, a ray of light, a ray of warmth peeps
                                                        over the hill,
Then there's a trickle and a dribble as the stream flows on
And the trees are swaying in the afternoon sun.

Rosie Garrard (13)
Colston's Girls' School

The (Not So) Happy Prince

There he stands, the statue of gold,
Encrusted with jewels, new and old,
Rubies, sapphires, gold and lead,
Is what he was made of.

He is not happy, although he should be,
He is covered in gold, but poor people he can see,
He cannot move, cannot help, he is stuck to the ground,
So he can see the sadness spreading around.

Here comes a swallow, flying far away,
'Tonight my bedroom is golden,' is what he was about to say,
When drip-drop. '*What!* There must be a leak,'
It wasn't raining, it was the statue!

For nights and nights, the swallow stayed,
Going back and forth with jewels,
Giving them to the poor and needy,
Doing what the prince said.

Soon the prince was brown and blind,
Because of his good deeds,
The swallow thought of his friends,
Darting through the reeds.

The swallow stayed with the prince,
Through all the winter months,
Soon the swallow could go no more,
And at the prince's feet he died.

Crack! went the prince's heart of lead,
And soon, he was dead,
The statue was taken down and was melted.

If you go to the rubbish dump,
And look you will see,
The body of a swallow and his cracked lead heart.

Emma Wear (13)
Colston's Girls' School

Death

Falling, falling,
Into an endless black pit.
Trying to get a grip,
So I can pull myself up.

Slipping, slipping,
Deep underground.
I try to scream,
But you can't hear a sound.

Beating, beating,
My heart beats faster.
I realise there's no way out,
I don't understand what this is all about.

Deeper, deeper,
It seems like forever.
When am I going to reach my destination?
Why am I being punished through this complication?

Drowning, drowning,
I'm being swallowed
Into a mysterious hole
And it's trying to rip out my soul.

Fighting, fighting,
My whole body shudders, with fear.
At the same time
I shed a tear.

Screaming, screaming,
I feel a shock of pain
Flowing through my veins.
I open my eyes and take my last breath
As I realise this is called death.

Shamuna Rahman (13)
Colston's Girls' School

A Shadow In The Mist

The girl's eyes twinkled
As she gazed at the moon,
The clouds surrounded the sky
Causing eerie shadows in the mist,
As they walked through the woods
She slipped her hand in his
And drew him in near.

Suddenly they jumped
As a shrilling scream
Blasted out,
They saw a man's shadow
In the distance.

Their pace increased,
They struggled and
Fought their way through bushes,
As they approached an open space
They stopped dead.

They saw a lifeless body
With a smile on her face . . . *dead*,
They turned around and froze.

Victoria Stokes (13)
Colston's Girls' School

The Intense Smile

As the queue drew us closer,
Our eyes caught as if we were all alone.
Although an unlikely lover
Passion was written all over the face,
A smile so golden the whole room illuminated.
How I longed to embrace!
I was left hung on every unspoken word of those lush lips
Although not moving,
The smile said it all and
I stared craving and loving.

Juliet Frimpong-Manso (13)
Colston's Girls' School

A Smile

A smile costs you nothing,
So smile all the time.
Whatever your language
Your smile means the same.
A smile can bring happiness
On a dull and dark day.
A smile is magical in
A mystical way.
A smile is enchanting
When it catches your eye.
A smile is spontaneous
Like lightning in the sky.
A smile is sparkling
In an interesting way.
A smile is the key to
Help you on your way.
Wherever you are,
Whatever you do,
Always remember to share a
Smile or two.

Hannah Vallin (13)
Colston's Girls' School

Searching For A Sign

She walked away from it all, and looked up to the sky
All she really wanted to do was run away and hide
She tumbled through the trees and rolled on the soft green grass
All she did was wait for time to pass
She took a few steps and breathed in the fresh air
She heard the chit-chattering of voices behind her
She ran in the other direction looking for a sign
Dropped her hands by her side and lay down and cried
She heard them coming nearer, so she stood up high
She spread her arms out wide and the wind ran through her hair
When the wind dropped she was no longer there.

Gabrielle Roberts (13)
Colston's Girls' School

Freedom

Flying and laughing,
Swinging and gliding,
Crashing and falling,
Happiness arising.

Splashing and chatting,
Clapping and tapping,
Dancing and singing,
Freedom passing.

Running and playing,
Twirling and swirling,
Jumping and singing,
Life just beginning.

Playing and waving,
Hopping and trotting,
Walking and skipping,
Birds that are singing.

Freedom is happiness,
Freedom is living,
Freedom is breathing,
Freedom is growing.

Or is this just a dream?

Sohaila Afify (13)
Colston's Girls' School

Loner Girl

I'm a loner girl.
No one knows how I feel.
They always stare
As if I'm not there, but
No one ever cares.
I'm paranoid, as they gossip, as they snigger,
Make fun of what I wear.
I make out I don't care,
But, deep inside I do.
I cry myself to sleep at night
Wishing I was someone else.

I'm a loner girl.
I wish I was someone else.
They always stare
As if I'm not there, but
No one ever cares.
I feel trapped, insecure, blocked out from the world,
As if I was in a box.
They hunt me down like a fox.
Daily the rumours go round.
All I want is a friend,
But, I'm a loner girl
And I guess I always will be.

Matisse Backler (13)
Colston's Girls' School

The Dance Of The River

Bubbling this way, that way, the other way
Forwards, backwards, faster, faster,
Up and down, round and round.
Chuckling, chugging, pulling, tugging.

Clinging. Holding then letting go and losing
Over and over, crashing and swirling,
On and on, bashing and hurling,
Clasping and grasping, frithing and frothing.

Again and again,
Splitting off and going on bounding,
Whooshing, slapping and splashing,
Dancing, laughing, cheerfully pounding.

Cold and penetrating, wishing and dreaming,
Exciting and fresh, carefree and streaming,
Further and further away she flows,
Where has she gone? No one knows.

Sarah Vernon (13)
Colston's Girls' School

Wild Horses

The ground trembles beneath my feet
As I hear the drumming beat.
A blurred silhouette on the horizon
A hundred stampeding horses,
Four hundred hooves
All hammering out the same steady beat.
They thunder past me,
Silken coats rippling,
Sweat dripping,
Mouths foaming white.
The air carries a piercing neigh,
In a second they're gone,
A flash wasn't long,
Wild horses won't get them to stay.

Florence McClelland (13)
Colston's Girls' School

A Walk In The Woods

My big boots shuffle through the crispy, crunchy winter leaves.
Frost hangs off the bare winter trees,
Birds are chirping,
The sun is creeping in through the tall trees,
Which almost touch the sky.
The squirrels scutter up trees, carrying round acorns,
Their bushy tails bouncing up and down,
My boots are muddy, hair a mess and I'm cold.
I blow out frosty air through my nose like a dragon,
And the pond at the very end of my journey has frozen over,
Glittering, gleaming in the early morning sun
And is covered in beautiful, different coloured lilies.
There are ducks quacking and searching for worms
Under the cold icy water.
I sigh and walk on home for a traditional cooked breakfast.
My mission accomplished.

Carla Ahmadi (13)
Colston's Girls' School

The Death Of Ideas

What is a poem
But the death of an idea?
A bright dancing spark
Lighting up the mind,
Torn away
And pinned onto paper
As a butterfly pinned onto cork.

What is a poem
But the death of imagination?
A sad, sorry sight
Trapped in its white lined cage,
Forever longing
To be free,
To light up the mind again.

Imogen Small (13)
Colston's Girls' School

The Shadow Behind Me

I walked through the alleyway,
In the middle of the night,
The rain started dripping,
Drip, drop, drip, drop,
I couldn't hear anything, except for that.
I looked behind me to see if anyone was there,
A man was following me,
Which I didn't really care.
I walked a bit faster,
The rain did too.
The man's footsteps were like,
Splish, splash, splish, splash,
But getting faster every minute.
I tried to run but I was too tired.
He touched me on my shoulder,
And burnt me like fire.
My heart was bumping,
Bump, bump, bump, bump,
Faster and faster.
I felt a rush of fire through me,
The man looked straight into my eyes,
My body went all numb.
He slapped me on my face.
I turned my face around,
I fell to the ground.
The hotness I felt from the pain.
Which felt like going down to Hell,
And passed out on the way.

Christine Vien (13)
Colston's Girls' School

The Storm

Splish,
Splosh,
Splish,
Splash,
The rain came down with a crash
And a flash
Of the lightning
Tightening,
Very, very frightening.
Hear the pitter-
Patter,
Pitter-
Patter,
It's the clatter
Of the feet
In the street
As they dodge
And they meet
And they run
And they seek
In the looming,
Glooming,
Dooming,
Booming
Hostile air.

Alys Fletcher (13)
Colston's Girls' School

Mistaken

She met with him at twilight
Upon the cobbled wall,
Her expression so happy, but why?
For he held none at all.

He was her lover
But not that her husband knew,
And he was going to pay the penalty for being with her
At the deadly hour of two.

Slowly and quietly he crept through the shadows
Holding a sharp-bladed knife,
But so carelessly was he in anger
That he mistook the lover for his wife.

The scream that filled the mountains high
Was deadly to the ear,
'Tis the wife who now lies dead beside the wall
Year after year.

Alex Bartlett (13)
Colston's Girls' School

The Lion

The lion is big,
The lion is strong,
The lion is cute
But the lion does wrong.

He wags his tail
And bares his teeth,
The lion looks sweet
But is wild beneath.

He can purr like a cat
And frolic in fun,
The lion seems playful
But can kill like a gun.

Elena Gugunava (13)
Colston's Girls' School

Lovers' Rendezvous

A spring in my step,
On my way,
A visit's in mind,
That's the plan for today.

As I come to see you,
My anticipation is burning deep,
My feelings are running high,
As I know I'll disturb your long sleep.

Our times in the past,
Have been so much fun,
It saddens me,
As I know no more will come.

Time to leave my love,
So proud and brave,
As I stand and walk
Away from your grave.

Emma Hatton (13)
Colston's Girls' School

Black Cats

Cats as black as the night
Tend to give people a terrible fright.
Skulking around long after dark,
See their eyes as you go through the park.

Gleaming yellow like rays of sun,
See their green pupils as they run,
Softly and carefully
And half wearily.

Howling and yowling
As they go prowling.
No animal ever dares go out
When the black cats are about.

Naomi Holloway (13)
Colston's Girls' School

African Beauty

As you stare into the face of the wise old man,
You try to draw out all the years of wisdom,
In his eyes you see the many stories he has to tell,
Stories that have been told to every ear that has passed his way,
But how many stories?
His face bears a mark for each one.

As you stare into the face of the wise old man,
In his eyes you see the many traditions of his ancient tribe,
The culture of his country,
And his family's way of life,
But how many traditions?
His face bears a mark for each one.

As you stare into the face of the wise old man,
In his eyes you see the crafts that he has learnt,
The crafts he has passed on to the many that have lived,
And those who have learnt have passed the crafts on,
But how many crafts?
His face bears a mark for each one.

Hattie Lister (13)
Colston's Girls' School

The Beach

Waves crashing against the rocks,
Birds gathering in screeching flocks,
The sun shining its dazzling rays,
Friends on the shore overlooking the bays,
Sandcastles standing constructed with pride,
Scuttling crabs trying to hide,
Buckets and spades sprawled everywhere,
Seaweed scattered here and there,
Rock pools filled with multicoloured fish,
It's every child's dearest wish.

Katie White (13)
Colston's Girls' School

I Can't Help It

I can't help them,
The tears that roll down my face.
My father still beats me
As if it's a race
To see how many times he can hit me,
Just to keep the peace.

I can't control it,
The way my father feels about me.
I try my best, I really do,
But my dad just doesn't see
How unhappy I am,
How unhappy he's making me.

I can't help them,
The tears that roll down my face,
For my father has hit me
And the blood seeps like lace
Down my cheekbones,
Down my face.

Natalie Parker (13)
Colston's Girls' School

A Cold Night

It was a dark, cold night
When they were walking through the park.
Yet nobody was in sight,
All that could be heard was the fizzing of some sparks.

They held each other tight,
They whispered as they crept around.
Soon they would be in for a fright,
They could no longer hear a sound.

They froze; their legs began to shake,
And then they saw a shadowy gloom,
Glistening from far across the lake,
Was this a sign of their doom?

Megan Pardoe (14)
Colston's Girls' School

The Dance Of The Flame

Embers flicker quietly here where a great fire once danced,
The fire that once here danced, it whirled, it twirled,
It jumped and flickered, it swayed, it played,
It took everything under its warm blanket,
It danced with the leaves,
Swayed with the breeze,
It licked the trees,
It teased the stream,
It followed the path, trying to make friends with the animals,
But the animals did not want to play,
They ran away.
The fire danced on, taking more trees
And leaves under its warm blanket,
But men gave the fire water, the fire steamed in rage
But couldn't dance on,
Now embers crackle quietly where the great fire once danced.

Jade Jetley (14)
Colston's Girls' School

Loneliness

As she sat in silence, loneliness swept over her like waves over sand.
She had no friends in school; they all thought she was strange.
Everyone in her class talked behind her back,
Muttering, murmuring, but stopping the moment she arrived.
At home she was miserable; there were too many rows.
Her parents had split like stars at opposite ends of the galaxy
And her dad had no job.
She was drowning in silence and sorrow.
Memories encircled her, bad, bad, bad.
The silence was unbearable, threatening to choke her;
The silence was unbearable, not a whisper, not a shout:
A silence so complete and thorough even the wind had no voice
As it blew through the trees and bushes.
She sat in silence and thought, *woe betide me if I live in such misery.*

Elizabeth Evans (13)
Colston's Girls' School

Different Smiles

I have lots of different smiles:
A smile for school,
A smile for home,
A smile for shopping,
A smile for friends,
A smile for babies,
A smile for new people,
A smile for family,
A smile to cover up when I'm sad,
But there's one smile, just one
That I have no control over,
That is the smile for when I'm really happy,
It stretches across my face
And it feels so good.

Charlotte Lonsdale (13)
Colston's Girls' School

The Demon Drink

He picks up the deadly bottle once more,
But what is going through his mind?
What about us?
What will we do
When the alcohol finally pulls him under?
All I see are empty bottles
And smashed ones from the never-ending rows.
Yet again he chooses the drink over us
As the poison lures him back, again.
I love him and yet I hate him.
I love the sober, controlled him,
But I'm scared of the out of control
Drunk he so often turns into.
So many times he tried to fight it,
But in the end the demon drink just
Got the better of him.

Stephanie Kelley (14)
Colston's Girls' School

I'm Tired Of Running . . .

I'm tired of running, my legs are aching, it's frustrating,
I hear the thoughts banging in my head asking,
When's this running going to stop?
Why am I always in a strop?
When will they stop treating me like dirt,
Stop making me hurt?
Can't they see I'm in pain, sustaining the strain?

I'm tired of running, I seem to have no fate,
All I feel is hurt, am I just a big debate?
Why do I have to be the one that has to run?
How come they get all the fun?
What's wrong with me? Was I not meant to be?
I'm tired of running because when I look back
And see all I am running away from is me . . .

I'm tired of running, my heart's still burning,
It's very frightening, but no one cares,
Because no one knows . . . all I get is stares . . .
Is it too late to retaliate and set the record straight?
But what can I achieve? All these people seem to be so naïve.
My life is just like a sad song and yet so damn long,
All I do is run along . . . and tag along.

I feel like an outcast, someone who doesn't belong,
It just feels so wrong and yet the feeling's so strong,
Should anyone have to feel like this?
Having no one even realise you exist?
I haven't done anything to hurt anyone
I've reached the point where
I cannot bear this despair, it's all so unfair.

If only these people would let me be
They'd soon see I'm no one but me.

Sharon Mundozo (14)
Colston's Girls' School

Deception

Her life was full of shadows,
Which she loved to dare,
Hiding here and there.
She knew she must leave;
This burden was too hard to bear.
As she ran through the wood
She felt a shiver down her hood.
She glanced from side to side,
This was meant to be her sanctuary,
Where would she now hide?
She knew she must be quick,
For just the thought of him made her sick.
There were eyes everywhere,
She could feel their disapproving glare.
Suddenly she stopped,
At that point her heart dropped,
He was standing there amongst the night,
So, she ran, ran to the light.
She couldn't take the deceit,
What would he say if he knew she was a cheat?
Her secret now will never be known,
She rejoiced with a groan.
For she had reached her destination,
And thrown herself off with a slight sensation,
So she lay there a gentle smile upon her face,
With her enemy towering over her, knowing he had lost the chase.
There her enemy wept and cried,
'What is the point of life?'
For he had lost his wife.
So now the secret is buried at the bottom of the sea,
Along with her and also he.

Saliha Mahmood (14)
Colston's Girls' School

Depression

Depression's where there's no way out
And everything has so much doubt.
All you feel is regret
But all you want to do is forget
The pain that they have caused you,
The fact they don't adore you,
The physical pain
That drives you insane
When there's no one there
And they don't even care.
No one ever notices you,
They just want to forget about you,
But all the hope has gone
And it's taken you so long, but
Just look beyond
You'll see there's someone who's longed
For you to come along,
Someone who feels the same
As if they too are going insane,
And there's no one to blame
For that horrible pain.
All you have to do is forget
All those people who made you upset,
Because, now they've put you through the test,
It's obvious that you're the best!

Jane Holmes (13)
Colston's Girls' School

Childhood

Plip, plop, splash,
Whoosh, screams of annoyance.

Flitter, flutter,
Swoop, scoop,
Pounce, bounce,
Catch it, miss it,
Let it go.
Scrunch, crunch,
Jump, thump,
Swirl, twirl,
Catch it, miss it,
Let it go.

Pose, position, stretch,
Lift up and lift down.
Test once, test twice.
Pose, position, stretch,
Flip, flap, fly!

Forwards, backwards,
Forwards, backwards,
Backwards, forwards,
Jump, thump,
Forwards, backwards,
Backwards, forwards,
Jump, thump.

Hannah Hoskins (14)
Colston's Girls' School

Eighty-Something

These eyes aren't what they used to be,
Opal-green and sparkling,
Able to peer across the fields of barley,
Able to pierce with a stare,
Enchanting men into my hands.

These ears aren't what they used to be,
So small and perfectly shaped,
No plastic gadgets and batteries blocked them
From the eyes of the world,
Able to hear gossip from yards and onwards.

These lips aren't what they used to be,
As red as cherries and firmer than unripe mangoes,
Able to spread kisses round the village,
And gain me the nickname 'hot lips'.

But now my eyes are dreary,
From viewing the world's sorrows,
My ears are scarred
From hearing the world's wars and worries,
My lips are thin, colourless and untouched,
At the age of eighty-six still lingers the memory
Of my very first kiss.

Anoushka Campbell (14)
Colston's Girls' School

A Lover's Parting

Her hair shone in the moon's light
As she lay upon the bay,
Waiting for her one true love
Day after day.

For she came here on the beach
Upon twilight every eve,
For the lover she had once loved
Now she deeply grieved.

It was twenty years ago
They came here hand in hand,
With a lover's kiss they parted,
One on sea, one on the land.

He sailed into the distance
On the rough and stormy seas,
Her handkerchief grasped tight
As she fell upon her knees.

Twenty years of sadness,
Twenty years of gloom.
Was to always grieve for him
Going to be her doom?

Lucy Webber (14)
Colston's Girls' School

The Morning Mouse

The golden sun rays pierce my eyes
And wake me from my sleep.
The emerald-green fields shine all around me,
Wet with morning dew.
I sense the soft swaying of the grass.
The morning wind ruffles my white sleek fur.
I feel my feet scrabbling over the solid ground.
My mouth fills with warm stringy skin.
The vast land, mountains, oceans stretch before me,
An opportunity.
I'm a small thread in a big tapestry,
I'm a little fish in a large pond,
I'm a young mouse in a huge world.

Joseph Hamlen (11)
Filton High School

The Panda

The forest floor, hard under my soft furry feet,
As the green grass rustles in the powerful wind
I stare all around me for miles,
All I see is beautiful brown bamboo sticks,
I was in bamboo heaven!
Screeches
Like chalk being dragged across a blackboard
Echoed around the forest,
The wax-like aroma
Filled the natural surroundings,
My mouth dribbled.
Turning to control myself
I turned my back
On the delicious scent of nourishment.

Gurveet Singarda (11)
Filton High School

Unreturned Love

As she walked by I felt my jaw drop,
As she sat down I felt my blood stop.
Later that day down at the park
I saw her swinging which made my heart spark.

Next day in school she made my face blush,
Until she flung by in a big rush,
That night on the bus
She made a big fuss,
Over her broken nail.

Then she looked back into my eyes
And turned back round only to cry,
Under the green huge tree,
Never for me to see!

Always right there
With her brown hair,
Longing for people to see,
She is the one for me.

David Dolan (11)
Filton High School

The Dolphin

I skim my way through the morning waves jumping up and down,
Swarms of blues, reds, greens and yellows brighten up the sea,
The sweet scent of my family circles me,
The sea below is a hive of noise,
The sweet splashes of the fish,
I sense danger before me,
A shark!
I've lost my family,
                    I'm lost!

Melanie Chapman (11)
Filton High School

Otters Of The River

Another day, I wake to crying pups.
Another day, I struggle up the muddy bank.
Another day, I glide through the crystal river.
Another day, I have fish for tea.
Another day, my pups cry for their lunch,
Their voices loud, soft and gentle.

I struggle through the raging currents,
I feel alone.
I push myself to go faster,
To join the other otters,
To be included in their group
They swim away,
I feel alone.

I live the life of a lonely otter,
Or I did.
Now I have
One best friend.
We do everything together,
We glide together,
We feed our pups together,
We do everything together,
Now I live the life of a very happy otter.

Rebecca Collins (11)
Filton High School

Love

Love is the smell of strawberries,
Love is the smell of sweets,
Love smells of cherries.

Love is doves flying high,
A love boat floating down through the river.

Love tastes of chocolate,
Love tastes of doughnuts,
Love tastes sweet and warm.

James Roe (11)
Filton High School

The Hospital

Doors flying, people screaming,
Doctors running, nurses scooting.

Clickety-click, trolleys being wheeled
Nee-nor, nee-nor, ambulances rushing!

Very ill people in intensive care,
People in resuss, people being sutured.

Clickety-click, trolleys being wheeled
Nee-nor, nee-nor, ambulances rushing.

People in physio in a swimming pool,
People sitting still for an X-ray.

Clickety-click, trolleys being wheeled
Nee-nor, nee-nor, ambulances rushing.

Newborn babies in their cots,
Crying children in the children's ward.

Clickety-click, trolleys being wheeled,
Nee-nor, nee-nor, ambulances rushing.

People smiling as they go home,
I hope that's me very soon!

Catherine Bailey (12)
Filton High School

Love Poem

Have you ever wondered
How much you mean to me?
Have you ever wondered
Why roses are so bright?
Have you ever wondered
How love boats swim around?
Have you ever wondered
If romance is true?
Have you ever wondered
If passions will fly by?

Amy Smurthwaite (11)
Filton High School

Lizard Life

Lizard scaly and spiky,
Basking in he sun.
Sleeping in shelter,
Dreaming things that's fun.

Wake up in the morning,
Running across the desert.
Searching for little bugs,
Eating them in pleasure.

Laid round new eggs,
Hatching any day.
When they finally crack open,
They'll look different in every way.

Clawprints in the sand,
Detailed and tiny.
Their tails and legs are smooth,
All their scales are nice and shiny.

Roxanne Perkins (11)
Filton High School

Love

Love makes me happy,
Love makes me fight,
Love makes me passionate,
Love makes me bright,
But best of all love makes me feel right.

Love tastes sweet,
Love brings heat,
When I lose it, it makes me weep.

Love is joyful,
Love is fun,
Love is special,
So come on everyone!

Tom Williamson (11)
Filton High School

Feelings

What's the point of living? I can't see or hear,
I can't see the beautiful colours or hear
The birds sing.

I think to myself, why was I born?
Why was I put onto Earth?
I can't see the world so what's the point?
Or maybe I was put onto Earth
To suffer for a reason.

My life would never change
If I even cried
And screamed!
I never knew life would be
So hard, it's hopeless!

But I was wrong, my life did
Change, a wonderful
Person came, it was like
She was sent for only me!
It's a miracle, she taught
Me how to sign, it seemed
Like I could actually talk to her!

She was the first person I
Could communicate to
With my hands, I thought
It was hopeless until she came,
She was the one person for me.

Rahat Ahmed (11)
Filton High School

The Witches

They're as ugly as a rotten fish,
Their hair is as greasy as a frying pan,
Their noses are as pointed as a pen
And their eyes are like long black tunnels.

David Stafford (13)
Filton High School

Dolphin

The swishing seaweed
Swaying side to side as if it's
Being pushed by a powerful wind,
Ice-blue sea surrounds everything.
The crystal clear water is full with
Multicoloured fish swimming freely.
The rocks sitting alone
On the golden brown sand.
The freezing cold water skimming my back
As it darts to and fro.
I smell the large, crystal, salty water,
The beautiful fish as they swim near me.
I can hear rocks smashing
Together, it is like
Aeroplanes crashing,
Bang, bang, bang.
The other sea animals
Contacting each other.
Boats sink like people
Gulping down a huge glass of water.
I touch the rocks as I swim by
Scratching my smooth sides.
I feel the luscious smooth water
Gliding along my body,
Swish, swish, swish.

Amy Dunning (11)
Filton High School

The Little Man

I know about a man
As small as a pan
His name is Dan
He laughs at his gran
Then got blown away by a fan
Now he's a squished little man!

Connor Coles (11)
Filton High School

Who Am I?

I roam the plains of Africa,
I have four legs and a tail,
My colours are yellow and black
And my sharp teeth are deadly.

I like to kill carefully
So my prey doesn't get away,
It's hard to keep up with gazelles
Because they're as fast as me.

I am one of the fastest animals
In the whole of the world,
I like the smell of warm fresh flesh
Because it's my favourite food.

Who am I?

Chris Lewin (11)
Filton High School

Who Am I?

I live in the big blue sea,
I see rainbow flapping fish,
They make a wall around me.

A colourful wall,
A beautiful wall,
I see light on the surface,
There is a scent of warm sand.

My belly starts to rumble,
I'm hungry,
I look for some krill,
I see a bunch of them,
They are like grapes,
Plump, juicy ones.

Najwa Bassir (11)
Filton High School

Christmas Eve

Christmas is coming,
It's nearly here
With Santa Claus
And his flying reindeer.

What shall I have?
What shall I have,
PlayStation, TV or
A new bath?

Not for me
Obviously,
For Mum and Dad
(They smell real bad.)

It's Christmas Eve,
I just can't wait
For tomorrow to come,
Fun for everyone.

Lauren Nutt (11)
Filton High School

Wild Tiger

The baking African sun burnt my delicate fur.
As I prowled through the crisp grass
I was looking for my target,
I heard a growl from my stomach,
I was hungry.
Suddenly I spotted my target,
An unknowing gazelle didn't smell my presence.
My back legs bounded out the long grass,
As my claws sank in I felt the gush of blood hit my lips.
My mouth opened wide and out came a roar of triumph,
I am Tiger, hear my roar!

Richard Higbey (11)
Filton High School

Fireworks

A cold night in November, a crowd gathering round
People getting excited, the children getting restless.
The sky a black canvas painted all black.

Then suddenly the canvas dull no more.
Yellow, red, orange, green and blue, every colour imaginable
The crowd waving, looking up into the glittering sky.

The fireworks all gone now, nothing in the sky.
Once again a blank canvas
And then time for the bonfire.

Guy Fawkes at the top, sparks glittering,
Blazing fire warming up the sky.
The crowd amazed, absolutely stunned.

Time to go now, no one wants to leave.
The children amazed or even stunned.

Amy Wakeford (11)
Filton High School

The Moonlight Trance

I stare into the night,
There's a groovy light in the sky.
I'm the light,
I'm going into the night,
I'm in a trance, a trance I tell you.
Destruction all over again,
All over the night,
By the groovy light, the sun has risen.
The trance is over
And the sun is brightly lit,
And the trance bids you goodbye
Until sunset.

Christopher Wide (11)
Filton High School

My Love Story

I give you chocolates
I give you gifts
I give you everything,
As long as you return,
A simple bit of love back.

He gave me my love
Just like I asked,
He gave me gifts
And kissed me too,
Then, he disappeared just like that!

I found a new man,
Sweet, charming and cute.
He gave me gifts,
Unlike the first,
Our love is like a kite,
Flying high in the sky.

Now I have a daughter
As sweet as can be,
She's mine and my man's
No one else's.
She will grow up,
To be like me!

Rachael Nicholls (11)
Filton High School

Nightmare

I had a terrible nightmare last night,
It had rats on flying mats,
My house being eaten by mice,
I can't say anything else,
Why?
There's a giant mouse . . .
On top of my house.

Hazel Gowen (11)
Filton High School

Britain's Beautiful Side

Countryside, countryside,
Why are you so nice?
Answer me, answer me,
Why are you so nice?
Because of my trees boy,
Because of my trees,
Tell me more, tell me more,
Why are you so nice?
Because of my grass boy,
Because of my grass,
Tell me more please, lots more,
There is one more thing,
One more thing you must know,
Tell me, tell me please!
Very well my surroundings,
The pigs, the horses,
The cows, the ducks, the goats,
That's it, are you sure?
That's it boy, that's all.

Jason Dixon (11)
Filton High School

Teachers

Some scary, some mad
But some are quite fab
They dive in the school
Which is not very cool
Hey! What can I say?
They will just have to pay
I hope the day
Will come in May
That they will confess
That they are a mess.

Matthew Cooper (11)
Filton High School

A Sparkling Life

As they wade through the glistening oceans
the starfish plunge down
while smiling at the amazing creation.

They jump to get clean air while
the exhilaration of the waves lapping against them.

The sun glittered in the ocean
like pretty little lights
lit up in the blue sparkling water.

When dolphins jump they're so happy
they try to stay still up in the air,
but they end up back in the water.

It's a hard-working day for the sea creatures
as they tuck up to sleep for another amazing day.

Sammy Mountford (11)
Filton High School

Shadow Snake

The warm moist soil of the Amazon
Eased and calmed me into a solitude rest.
My eyes catch movement, it was prey
More succulent than the best.

Its odour alerts and arouses me
Drawing me, delayingly closer
It grew into contact, it put up a fight
But its blood soon trickled from my mouth
Its struggle hard to endure.

I then slithered into thick murky shadows
In wait of another . . .

Ben Turner (11)
Filton High School

Life Is A Wonderful Thing

I woke up this morning got out of my bed
I looked in the mirror then I got myself dressed,
With a stretch and a yawn and a scratch of my head.

'Life is a wonderful thing,' I said
'Life is a wonderful thing.'

I went downstairs and what did I see?
Bees and the blossom and the birds in the trees.

'Life is a wonderful thing,' I said
'Life is a wonderful thing, ha ha
Life is a wonderful thing.'

I went in the kitchen and Mum said to me,
'Son you better tidy your room.'
There was a knock on the door and it was for me, phew!

'Life is a wonderful thing,' I said
'Life is a wonderful thing, ha ha,
Life is a wonderful thing, ha ha.'

Hayley Clifford (12)
Filton High School

Air Hunter

I'm released, I flap, I soar
Catching their scent all juicy and warm
I see them jumping up and down
Scampering as my partner
The ferret scampers towards them.

Swoop, grab, kill, return
No congratulations to me
This is my lifetime job
It may not be glamorous
But it's what I'm born to do.

Jack Rice (11)
Filton High School

Seasons' Feelings

Spring is jealous,
jealous of summer,
summer is warmer,
with flowers of summer.

Summer is in love,
with the colour of its flowers,
red, purple, pink and blue,
all of them are brand new.

Autumn has hatred on winter,
it is cold and frosty,
but autumn is leafless,
and dull!

Winter is a murderer,
it is a murderer for cold
no trees, no leaves
only a white blanket.

Sophie Vardon (12)
Filton High School

The Cat

As I was walking,
The wonderful scent of the grass,
Wind was blowing fiercely on my tail,
I was walking back to the barn,
I was chasing a mouse!
Charging,
Scratching,
The smell of blood,
I leapt at the fickle mouse,
I scratched and scratched,
Dead.

Mack Johnson (11)
Filton High School

Autumn

The green leaves rustle in the wind,
They are all different colours,
Green, brown, red and black.
Crunch and *crack* when you step.

Silence as you walk,
But when you get to a leaf
That is red or black,
Crack! Then silence again.

They gently fall, swiftly,
Onto the grass without a sound
Crack, it's just a cat.

Now the rain has come
Everything is wet,
Now the grass is all muddy,
Slug, slug.

Matthew Grey (11)
Filton High School

Dolphins Of The Ocean

The calling and singing of whales
Surrounding me like predators
In the distance I see a shark
Fiercely attacking its prey

The smell of warm, red blood
Floating through the waves
I feel the fish brushing past me
Like the bristles on a brush

The taste of lunch still in my mouth
Mmm fish
Thousands of multicoloured fish
Surrounding me in a kaleidoscope of colours.

Shauna Brain (11)
Filton High School

My Grandad

My grandad was so nice,
He bought me some mice.
He played cards with me,
I beat him two, three.

He made me laugh,
He gave me a bath.
It makes me cry,
Because time has flown by.

Now he has gone,
I feel that's not on.
I miss him lots,
He comes out tops.

My grandad was so nice,
He bought me some mice.
He played cards with me,
I beat him two, three.

Naomi Jones (12)
Filton High School

As Cute As Can Be

It's an animal as cute as the rain,
Its fur as soft as the bottom of my hair,
The little nose feels just like snakeskin,
Doesn't eat much, fit and thin,
A good little animal it usually goes yap, yap, yap!
Just as the door roars tap, tap, tap!
Its fur can be ginger, black, brown and white,
What a cutie she's a sight,
It sleeps whenever it wants,
But it's not lazy can't you see,
It's a dog as cute as can be.

Katie Leck (11)
Filton High School

Murder Love

The storm was raging
Death was polluting the air
You could see her eyes
You could see it in her hair.

She set off to find her lover
To kill him then he would always
Be hers forever and ever.

Soon she arrived at her lover's feet
Whispering soft strange words like prayers
Then stab once! Stab twice!
He fell to the floor with all the mice.

She took his heart and held it in her hand
And said, 'I hated you with the hate of Hell.
But I loved him with the love of God
Now you're mine forever locked away in my heart.'

Jamie Mitchell (12)
Filton High School

The Hand Of Destiny

The brown, dotted outside palm,
White knuckles as they ever are,
The white skin leading up to my nails,
The pink, pale nails which are as small as a bar.
I turn my hand,
I see, I see, I see my veins wandering round my palm,
All my destiny in my palm.
The pink palm leading to my whitish fingers,
The pen nearly on my fingertips.
Then I get to the top of my fingers
Red-hot as they always are begging for water.

Kai Smith (11)
Filton High School

Spain

The sun glistening down on the nice calm sea.
The waves splashing on my face.
The banana boat chucking me off and tipping.
The cave houses dark and cold.
The nightclubs raving with loudness
Spain's lovely villas and pools
Sun shining down on the people
Spain, Spain lovely Spain.

Chris Winstone (11)
Filton High School

Stars!

As I look up and even higher in the sky,
I see stars as graceful as a butterfly,
I love the way they sparkle
In the moonlight sky,
But I really hate it when they flutter by.
The stars are our country
Above us they stay,
But I love the stars like
Horses love hay!

Abigail Chodkiewicz (11)
Filton High School

Animals

Pigs find it hard to crawl.
Tigers are frightening zebras.
Leopards are as shiny as straw.
Elephants are as fat as a car.
Ants are miniature bulls.
Emus are as thin as a bar.
Horses are like houses afar.

Jade Weston (11)
Filton High School

A Gate To Another World

Hours and hours I looked out my window,
It's a gate to another world, no, a portal.
I really admired this massive fire who let me go through.
I fell through the window and landed in a meadow.
There I lay for an hour and a whole day,
Undiscovered not even covered.
There I lay asleep in hay,
Only to be discovered the next day.
Dead, not alive, I lay.

Gethyn Ulyatt (11)
Filton High School

SS Great Britain

The ship sails great,
across the wide-eyed lake.

The mast stands high,
as the sailors pass by.

The crew look grand,
as they look for land.

And I, I sit and watch in luxury!

Alex Leggett (11)
Filton High School

Space

Space is like a lake, flowing on forever and ever,
When suddenly, it stops.
No one knows where and why
The stars light up the black, lonely emptiness.
The planets like a tree's collection of leaves,
Rustling in the breeze.
The sun is a great ruler, ruler of the light
And leaves and trees and breeze.

Diana Sakota (11)
Filton High School

Autumn

Leaves are falling
Misty morning
Smoky breath
As cold as death.

Dark nights
Give you the frights
Hedgehogs are eating
Ready for sleeping.

Squirrels gathering nuts
Frozen water butts
Cobwebs glitter
Cold and bitter.

Adam Gleeson (11)
Filton High School

Dogs

The dog's hair is smooth as tiles,
The nose is so wet, it's like it just rained,
Its tongue is rougher than brick.

It runs as fast as a bicycle,
They come in all sizes
And love going for walks.

Cats steer clear of this beast,
Because if they do not,
They could meet a very sticky end.

Dogs are beautiful animals
And are man's best friend,
As they are mine.

Adam Turner (11)
Filton High School

Keo The Dog

I could smell
Danger,
Fierce,
Smoke.

I could feel
Spiky rocks,
Wooden door
Vibrating.

I could see
Smoke,
Flames,
Shadow.

I could hear
Screaming,
Shouting,
Beating.

I could taste
A bitter smoke,
Danger.

Steven Mitchell (11)
Filton High School

I Know A Friend Called Mike

Bristol is where I live
I think it is the sieve.
It's got a zoo fit for a king
And the animals surely don't ming
Oh and it's got a skate-park
And it's quite a lark.
I wouldn't give it up for the world
Because Bristol is where I live.

David McCann (11)
Filton High School

Time

Clocks ticking
men drinking when time rolls by,
birds singing
trees waving whilst time rolls by,
humans walking
planes flying whilst the flies precious time of destiny keeps ticking
and the time is beating on,
people working, children playing as the time carries on,
longer and longer till the day runs out,
another day, another day whilst the time is early and awake,
people dreaming, cats and dogs sleeping
as the time is nearly run out,
people walking, birds are about to sing in the early dusk
of the morning, another day has started
and the time has started once again.

Danny Reed (11)
Filton High School

My Teacher

Our teacher is a mad old mop,
I swear he is not human
And if you see him you will drop
And see that he's a blue man.
If he walks into the class,
He'll only cause a scene
And if you choose to rip up grass,
He'll shock you with his laser beam.
This morning I sat up in bed
And put on the TV,
They said that my teacher's dead
And now I'm full of glee!

Michael Rowsell (11)
Filton High School

A Cold Winter's Evening

The warm fire is burning
The winter's evening is cold
I gaze through my frozen window
The snow is softly falling
Falling and resting on the hard ground
As the sky darkens
I see a white sheet being
Laid across the houses
I hear a dog barking
Howling at the snow
I take it in silently
Knowing that in the morning
It will be destroyed
When the children come out to play.

James Ashdown (11)
Filton High School

Dear Little Tobin

I don't know what to say
but little Tobin isn't here to stay.
From his mum and dad's love
he's a little angel up above.

We go to visit him sometimes
and all we see is a gravestone
and his new friend frog who we see
every now and then.

He now comes and visits
my auntie Emily, Uncle Steve,
Rioja and baby Deya to say
'Hello and goodnight,'
and he doesn't want to give them a fright.

Jessica Andrews (11)
Filton High School

If I Were A Dolphin - Can You Guess What I Will Sense?

In cold, icy water, hungry sharks,
Sly and slowly spy on every little move,
Prey of it it makes.
Out of the corner of my eye, I see seaweed,
Splashing multicoloured from little fish only just awake!
Seals splashing on the icy water all I can say is -
Beware of electric eels.

It's coming, smashing salty water and sandy mud,
Can you smell it?
Blood, poor creatures caught, sharks eat,
I can sense blood.
The oil is terrible, always polluting water.

Waves clashing, waves clashing
Through the boats, speedboats
Making water colder
I wish I had a coat.

When I swam, seaweed and lily pads stirred
Together like spaghetti Bolognese, hmm!
Fish I eat when I am hungry,
Run, run I am after you soon.

Lazy water swayed side to side
As it splashed against my back,
Seaweed, waving and saying, 'Please don't put me in a sack!'

Morgane Foster (11)
Filton High School

The Homeless Poem

I am homeless and I don't really care
Looking at people I can't help but stare
They all have money and I ask for some spare,
They always look away as if I'm not there.

Jordan Estcourt (12)
Filton High School

Under The Sea

Deep beneath the ocean,
Corals lie untouched,
Not one bit of commotion,
Dull colours - not much!

Slightly higher above,
Signs of beautiful fish,
As soft and smooth as fluff,
Though they won't end up in a dish!

Merging into sunlight,
Liveliness is all around,
Sharks giving squid a fright,
Sharp teeth for which they're renowned!

Now at the sparkly surface,
Dolphins come in and out,
Life out here is utter bliss,
So long as we're not about!

Jyothi Pillay (12)
Filton High School

Autumn

Playing in the crackly, crumbly leaves,
Throwing them up and down and around.
See the fog in the distance, we will have a chill
Yes we will.
Walking about with my hat and gloves
Dancing around making a big bang.
I have a break and have a warm drink, ahh.
I sit down for the evening watching the smoky air rise.
I sit there and watch the yellowy, browny, goldy leaves fall.
I go to bed and pretend to be dead.
I see the see-through ice covers my window to keep them strong
Autumn!

Shelly Janes (11)
Filton High School

Seasons

Silent snow lies blanketing the top of the Earth,
Winter has brought its short days and coldness.
The ground hardens and puddles turn to ice,
All around looks beautiful like a picture.

With subtle changes now it becomes spring,
Pink confetti blossoms on trees.
Lambs run joyfully round the fields,
Soon it will be Easter, new life is here.

Summer comes with its boiling bright sun,
Holiday tourists crowd onto the beach.
Splashing in the freezing sea,
Or sleepily lying developing a tan.

Autumn falls upon us next,
Orange, red and brown leaves decorate the ground.
Children collect shiny smooth conkers,
Prickly hedgehogs search for shelter.

This never-ending cycle repeats itself,
Each year bringing winter, spring, summer and autumn.
A variety of colours and scenes,
Each special in its own different way.

Natasha Cameron (12)
Filton High School

Autumn

Leaves falling down
Not making a sound
Making smoke
Like Lisa poke
Playing outside making a lot of sound
You will be all cold
You'll wear yourself out

You will get a chill, yes you *will*.

Charlotte Done (11)
Filton High School

My Best Friend

Her long brown hair flows as she moves,
Her green eyes sparkle in the sunlight.
Her tanned legs shine as she moves gracefully,
Her smile lights up a room.

She looks so happy all the time,
Like her life's one big smile,
She brightens up my day,
Every time she is near.

She has so many clothes,
Her wardrobe's like a mall,
Each day she looks so pretty,
Like she's come from a salon.

Her nails are so cool,
Like she's just had a manicure,
Her long, dark lashes flutter with each blink,
Like a hummingbird in motion.

She is so cool
And so understanding.
I'm lucky to have her
And she's my best friend.

Rebecca Dale (12)
Filton High School

Autumn

Golden leaves
Bare trees
Flowers dying
Beauty's crying
Animals sleeping
Mr Frosty is not weeping.

Ryan Jacobs (11)
Filton High School

Love Poem

You are my desire,
My very fire, you are in my soul.
Roses cannot show my love for you.
I love you,
You are my soulmate,
You're beautiful that's for sure, you're so pure.

My love cannot be shown,
Be mine my valentine.
I'm full of lust,
You must kiss me,
You must, you must,
My love is here,
You are near.

Connor Broughton (11)
Filton High School

Love Is Sweet

Love, love sweet as a rose
Love is happiness when you think it
Love is passion and romance
Red and white shows it's love

People say love is sweet
And looks like a rose
Love is wild and a heart
I wonder, is it true love?

Love looks like a dove
Love is soft
and love is true.

Ben Land (11)
Filton High School

Love Is . . .

Love is my passion,
Love is my soft spot,
Love is my strawberry lip balm,
Love is two rings entwined with each other.
Love is my wild side,
It's my crazy side,
It's what I wake up in the morning for,
Love is the affection that I respect.

Love is hatred,
It's cards and presents
And flowers
And so-called enjoyment.
However, love is you.

Millie Warrington (11)
Filton High School

All About The Sea

Smooth, scaly skin, swim through the big blue.
Big, furious, muddy teeth waiting impatiently.
Small, frightened fish sway gently, but nervously in the sea.
The rough texture of the colourful sea horse
Which sways side to side proudly.
The deadly jellyfish let out their powerful sting.
Brave divers quickly rush out of their boats.
They dive into the clear deep sea to see the colours of the fish.
As they swim in the sea they live happily as a big family.

Ashley Rew (11)
Filton High School

School!

This school is great,
But when I first got here,
I was pretty much a state,
Some time has gone by now
And doing pretty fine.
However I don't want to go
Through it again.

Rosie Passaway (11)
Filton High School

Trees

The trees are like a hand waving,
Waving from here to there
Saying hello as we pass.
They would hustle and bustle
All day and night.
Talking to one another
At the dead of night!

Chloë Choi (11)
Filton High School

Our Teacher

Our teacher's horrible,
The things he makes us do!

His face is horrible,
It's even worse than goo!

I don't think I'll make it,
Because of what he puts us through!

I hate him,
Even though he's new!

He treats us worse than a ship's crew!

Michael Selwyn (11)
Filton High School

A Rainbow

A wonderful thing has appeared in the sky,
High above the houses, high as high,
Multicoloured and beautiful,
Fantastic colours, bright and full.
A pot of gold is at the end,
Just over and past that magnificent bend.

Blue, orange, indigo, purple and yellow,
The sight of these colours makes the heart mellow,
Pink, red, violet and green,
All these colours, fit for a queen,
I try to reach out, and grab the bow,
If only it was lower, lower than low.

It arches high above the trees and flowers,
High above the castles and the towers.
Everywhere people are stopping to look,
At the colours in the sky, higher than the rook,
So when the sun and rain merge,
To smile and be happy, I have the urge.

Ellie O'Shea (12)
Filton High School

Love Poem

Desire your love
Cherish it
Deeply
Flowers symbolise it

Romance is everywhere
You can taste it, feel it and smell it

Passion, happiness, romance
all mean the same thing . . .
Love!

Emily Painter (11)
Filton High School

Ibiza

I sit upon the beach
And watch the sea so blue,
With golden sand around my feet,
I sit and watch the view.

I laze upon my sunbed
And watch the kids all play,
In the pool, on their floats and rings,
I could laze and watch all day.

I sit up in my seat
And watch the waiters serve food,
Balancing it on their arms,
We paid extra, a tip, not to be rude.

It's my go on the bungee,
I shoot up quite so far,
Watching people down below
All crowded in the bar.

I sit up in the aeroplane,
We travel back to England
To the rain and cold,
Leaving the sea and sand behind.

Michelle Holland (12)
Filton High School

Miss M Monster

My teacher is the most wonderful thing I've seen,
When she's angry she turns very green,
Otherwise,
She's spotty and stripy and polka-dot too,
Some people say she belongs in the zoo!

She wonders, she ponders,
She thinks and she winks,
My mate over there says
She lives in the sink!

Aleisha Talbot (11)
Filton High School

Love - The Happiest Thing

Love is sweet,
Love makes us strong,
Love is the colour of red,
Sometimes it makes me feel dead.

Love is the happiest thing,
Love makes everyone sing,
Love is just like a dove,
Everybody has a taste of love.

When night-time comes
And I'm alone in my bed,
I think of love
And that great white dove.

Now it is morning,
I still feel tired,
I feel as though I am going to collapse,
But love keeps me up for a brand new day.

Love keeps everyone alive,
It keeps us up in school,
Even though you are bored,
But when night comes,
Love speeds over my heart.

Keiron Jenkins (11)
Filton High School

Murder

Stabbed with a knife
Because he stole my ex-wife
And here I am in prison.

Prison cells are gloomy and dark
They feed me bread and water.

I wish I didn't do it now
I let my jealousy take me over.

Rochelle Bailey (12)
Filton High School

The World

Who made this wonderful world?
With its swirling waters and grassy land
And sky full of soaring birds,
The world you see from where you stand.

From the icy polar regions
To the dreary desert sand,
From the largest crowded nation
To the tiniest tropical island.

From the purple-headed mountain
To the Earth's deepest sea,
From the farthest barren plain
To the polluted city's plea.

See the fish swim, see the birds fly,
See the prey hiding from the cunning and sly,
See the phenomena of dawn and dusk,
See the elephants' great ivory tusks.

Who made this world,
This great, wide world?

It was He -
The one who gave us eyes to see
This all.
The Great Almighty!

Niranjani Prasad (12)
Filton High School

My Teacher

My teacher used to crawl
My teacher used to bawl
My teacher used to cry at night
Now my teacher is so tall
She hardly can recall
My teacher thinks she's different
But my teacher is not at all.

Terrie Harvey (12)
Filton High School

The Lonely Man

A man on his own
Without a home
Sat on the street
With his stinky feet.

People passed by
Looked to the sky
Holding their nose
Thinking of roses.

Went to his box
Put on his socks
Grabbed his coat
Then had a smoke.

Walked to a bin
Then found some gin
Fell asleep
Without a peep
And was never seen again.

Chris Lewis (12)
Filton High School

Nerds And Bullies And Grannies

Nerds are a disgrace to education
that's why you see bullies doing invasion and doing destruction
A mental granny comes along beating all the nerd gangs
                                           to Hong Kong
We get the blame and the shame, but she gets the fame
                                           and gets named
She sits on a pan and has a beer can and turns into a monk
But that's no problem I am a punk
She does all my dirty work with her fork
I sit and have a bit of pork and chewing a piece of cork.

Rizwan Ahmed (11)
Filton High School

The Love Thing

My love for you,
Is like a dove,
Soaring through the air,
The love has filled my heart.

You are the light of my life,
You fill me with happiness
That will never turn to sadness,
But to gladness.

I respect and worship you,
I'm addicted to you,
You're an infection that can't be cured,
I cherish and desire you.

I can't say how much I adore you,
The love boat doesn't give enough time,
I'll give you romance,
Please be mine!

Joe Sewell (12)
Filton High School

Prince Charming

You come to me at daytime hour to
give me the most beautiful flower.

And with your smile and your gentle eyes
you comfort me when tears drop from my eyes.

You would rescue me from the tallest tower
and come with courage and the greatest of power.

And when the day comes that you pull me near
and whisper words I'm happy to hear
then people dance and sing with glee that I can live happily
ever after with thee.

Natalie Fey (12)
Filton High School

The Window

I gazed into the crystal clear object,
It was hidden behind the dark blue sea,
Through is more blue with white fluff moving towards the right,
I gazed harder, it truly was a great sight,
There's more blue than white,
I looked down, I was really at a great height!
Then I looked further with all my might,
It sure was bright,
It says it's nowhere near night.

I pulled my head out and closed it,
I peeked through it, but I hit something hard,
It was made out of glass,
Not sure of its mass,
Looked down and there was grass,
A bus went past,
I looked fast,
Surely that's not the last.

My mum came up to me and said, 'It's a window.'

Hugh Wong (12)
Filton High School

You!

I love looking into your lovely eyes,
Every time you leave my heart nearly dies.
You are my true love,
Just like a white dove.
I wish I could be with you all of the time,
I still would if it was a crime

I

love

you.

Matthew Emery (12)
Filton High School

But Mum I Can't Sleep

'Turn off the light
Night-night
Hope the bed bugs don't bite
Night-night.'
'But Mum, I can't sleep.'

'Turn of the light
Night-night
Hope the bed bugs don't bite
Night-night.'
'But Mum I can't sleep.'

'Have a drink then dear
And please do not fear
Then . . .'

'Turn off the light
Night-night
Hope the bed bugs don't bite
Night-night.'
'But Mum I can't sleep.'

'Count sheep then dear
And don't worry I am near
Then . . .'

'Turn off the light
Night-night
Hope the bed bugs don't bite
Night-night.'
'But Mum I can't sleep.'

'Listen to the clock tick then dear
And please don't shed a tear.'

Daniella Pitkin (12)
Filton High School

My New Room

The builders Steven and Richard Long,
Who, as far as I knew could do no wrong.
They arrived one Monday morning at our door,
Van in tow and tools galore.

Our builders are full of well meaning,
But Richard put his foot through the ceiling.
After this, things got madder,
When they dropped the vacuum cleaner down the ladder.

They worked hard on my new loft room,
Even for all the moments of gloom.
A new toilet, a new roof and plenty of dust,
But after all, for my new room, this is a must.

Then one day along came Smudger, the plumber,
A nice guy, a friend of the builders but even dumber.
He measured the pipes and drilled the walls,
Unfortunately, like the vacuum he took a fall.

Everything is finished and the room looks splendid,
But the vacuum still isn't mended.
Steve gave us £50 towards the cost,
However, our Dyson is a terrible loss.

I helped my dad sand and varnish the wood,
The windows and doors looked really good.
I would like to paint the walls more and more,
But my dad said he 'didn't want splashes on the laminate floor'.

I'm looking forward to moving in,
Away from my brother who is a constant din.
I can hide things in this new room of mine,
Thank you lads for a nice design.

Lewis Evans (12)
Filton High School

My Secret Love

I see my love in the playground,
My eyes on him there is no sound.
He's the one I adore,
There's his girlfriend, my heart is sore.

Your hair is so sweet,
I'm floating off my feet.
I love the way he moves and walks,
Every time he lovingly talks.

I wish, I wish he would see me,
I wish, I wish he would know me,
I wish, I wish he would like me,
But I guess that'll never happen.

Hannah Theobald (12)
Filton High School

Death

Death is like a dagger stabbing you through your heart
time and time again.

Death is like a thousand bugs eating you inside
till you have no bones left in your body.

Death is like a tiger tearing you apart
in a matter of three seconds.

Death is like a million pins
sticking in your hands and feet.

No one likes death.

Jade Hallt (12)
Filton High School

Cheerleading

I started cheerleading early this year
Now I know how to cheer!
Stunts dance and round-off flicks
But don't forget those high, high kicks
We have to know how to do the splits
This is the queue for people to quit.

So now we are off to the USA
Competing and performing night and day.
Winning trophies, cups and all,
If we're not careful we might fall.
Give me a c-h-e-e-r-l-e-a-d-i-n-g
And what do you get? Cheerleading.

Daisy Pothecary (12)
Filton High School

Boredom

I'm sat at home I'm as bored as can be.
I'm laid on my bed with nothing to do.

I don't feel like eating, drinking or sleeping
And really need a friend to talk to.

School tomorrow I can chat and shout as much as I like
I might even play a game or two.

But right now I'm as bored as can be
And there's nothing on TV and nothing to do.

I might put some music on or play on my PS2
But right now I can't be bothered, there's just nothing to do!

Rachel Bennett (12)
Filton High School

When I'm Sat Here Alone!

When I'm sat here alone
I imagine my paradise with money
And a bed or a place to rest my head.

When I'm sat here alone
I hear ungrateful children
Laughing and screaming like hyenas.

When I'm sat here alone
I can taste the bitter nicotine in my mouth.

When I'm sat here alone
I can see people staring, sharing and caring!

When I' m sat here alone
I can smell the 'wonderful' smell of the sewers!

When I'm sat here alone
I can feel the stone-cold concrete
Beneath the wet, crunchy leaves.

Yes you've guess it
I'm homeless so spare some dosh
And my life will change.

Bethany Chodkiewicz (12)
Filton High School

Hand Of Fate

Pale pink piggies
pointing in all directions
wrinkly and old
like an old oak tree
nails rigidly cut
like hewn branches
lines of fate cross over
expecting an early death.

Fraser Chandler-Jones (12)
Filton High School

The Flying Pie

I'm Arnie Pie here in the sky
And what I'm seeing I'd rather die.
Look at this it's rather scary
A UFO above the dairy.
Oh no I'm sorry it's the wrong shape
It looks more like a flattened grape.
Oh the smell it's rather nice
It's blackcurrant and a certain spice.
It has four holes on the top
It's crushing every single crop.
Hey it looks quite expired
It's turning cows into vampires!
Oh my God it's a pie
Floating around the sky.
The flying cows think it's food
It considers it rather rude.
I'm Arnie Pie in the sky
I think I may die.
The pie is floating over the road
It looks like a heavy load.
Over the road the car did crash
Sending off a needle spike rush.
As it goes leaving rubble
Now this thing is asking for trouble.
Here comes the army parading through
Each one with a knife tattoo!
The bullet rebounds off its crust shell
And the whole city starts to yell.
People far away think it's great
To see our town's nasty fate!
I'm Arnie Pie in the sky
I'm the only one left alive.
The giant pie comes bombing down
I can't talk of the town
This giant pie, why not kill me?
Because I control it don't you see!

Daniel Packham (12)
Filton High School

Being Homeless

I sit still, slumped, silent, starving,
On the frozen floor beneath my feet.
My hands are frozen like icicles hanging from a roof.
The mean wind is like a pack of wolves howling, ripping me apart.
I sit around sluggishly in the day seeing the people bustling past me,
Some laughing.
At me?
I see the disgust in their faces,
Like I don't exist.
They sit in luxurious cafés sipping coffee.
I wish I could.
When I rise in the mornings I get greeted with the traffic thundering
Through the town.
It's like an alarm clock.
I get greeted with the horrific smell of the sewers
But on the other hand I can smell the cafés, they smell of coffee,
I wish I could afford a cuppa.
All I can taste is the bitter taste of nicotine
From the fag I smoked last night in my mouth still.
I could just imagine myself with a wedge of notes in a warm bed,
In a luxurious house, rather than a cold doorway, wouldn't you?
It's better being normal so don't become homeless.

Drew Tanner (12)
Filton High School

The Dolphin

I hear the whale's song
Beautifully echoing down the waters,
Swimming swiftly down the sea lanes
The water gliding over my back.
I taste the salty sea water
And the multicoloured fish
Forming a rainbow circle all around me.

Helen Short (12)
Filton High School

School

Teachers go mad when you give them looks,
They shout at you when you forget your books,
They give me a detention every day
And then they go mad when I say . . .
'That is so unfair!'

They give you homework like it's no big deal,
But I don't do it, instead I go up the field.
But then when I go into school,
I bump into Mr Hall, and he gives me another detention!

I'm always late in the morning,
Because tutor time is so boring,
But when the end of the day comes
I go out with my friends and actually have some fun!

Leah Sheppard (12)
Filton High School

Who Am I?

Surrounded by tall, looming tree trunks
With a large green bush on top.
What's that smell?
A putrid, sickly smell from the
Rotten bananas thrown on the dusty ground,
A gigantic sheet of velvet blue covering the sky.
The scorching hot sun glaring up above.
Yuck!
Treading through squelching mud
And rustling, dead leaves.
Sticks snapping,
Foul, disgusting animal droppings,
Laying on the bare ground,
Swinging from tree to tree.

Rosie Haynes (12)
Filton High School

Victorian Hell

Children on their way to work
As well as mums and dads
Children in factories
Watch out
Will they make the end?

Poor people finding scraps of cloth to wear,
While rich have dresses and suits,
Both are smelly as they do
Not take that many baths.

Disease running from one door to another,
Mostly caused by rats,
With Jack the Ripper on the loose,
No one goes to the doctor's.

It's the end of the day,
People come from work
And crawl into their small houses.

They find old books to light a fire,
As they sit and stir their broth,
The thin and watery soup.

Once finished crawl into bed,
Get ready for the next day ahead.

Sammi McLean (12)
Filton High School

Cool Clothes

Adidas is the best,
No wait, Nike is better than the rest,
Now hang on a minute Morgan is cool,
No FCUK is wicked, don't be a fool!

Wait there a second, what suits me the most
Is Gucci, I don't mean to boast!
But really it's up to you.
You can buy whatever you want, I don't care what you do!

Alice Fry (12)
Filton High School

Hot Apple Pie

When this small apple treat
Slides straight down your throat,
Its taste so luxurious,
Will surely make you float!

When the tasty little sweet
Falls down into your belly,
The voluptuous taste
Is better than your telly!

The small luscious snack
Is sure to make you try
To get another taste,
Of that hot apple pie!

Mitchell Cole (12)
Filton High School

Flowers

Flowers are the world to me,
The scent is strong,
As good as could be,
I feel the summer as I stand,
The flowers running through me.

Violet, daisy, tulip, rose,
All coming out in the sun,
They have all began to pose,
Standing out in the sun, having a bun,
I feel the flowers through me.

I see the clouds in the sky,
Darkening the happiness,
Raining, pouring on my tie,
I can feel the sadness,
I feel their spirits through me.

Hannah Vickery (12)
Filton High School

Tiger

The dry grass crunches,
Beneath my feet,
I run, run, the wind lashes
Against my face,
Got it the thing I wanted,
I bite and chew,
The skin is tough,
I rip and tear at it,
The red, warm blood
Around my jaw,
I lick it,
My eyes screw up
And my face becomes tight,
That's enough for one day,
I lay down on the brown, dying grass,
Waiting, waiting,
For my next victim.

Rebecca Suckley (12)
Filton High School

What Animal Shall I Have?

Dogs are cute and sometimes fluffy,
Cats are too when they are called Muffy.
I do not like mice because they're too small
And giraffes are just too tall.

I'd love to have an Easter bunny,
But not a hyena 'cause they are too funny.
Crocodiles' teeth are way too sharp
And I don't want an animal that plays the harp.

It is very easy to look after fishes,
But I could have a deer that licks the dishes.
It is very hard to pick one,
So I decided to phone my mum.

Emma Ryan (12)
Filton High School

The Boy Who Sits Next Door

I walk on by, I catch his eye,
Every time I see him I think I'll cry.
He turns the corner, I'm all alone,
I wish he'd call me on the phone.
The bell has gone, I walk to class,
My shoes get stuck in muddy grass.

He sits next door, I yawn as my class is a bore,
My jaw drops, as he looks at me.
My cheeks turn red as I stare ahead,
The boy who sits next door, I adore.
His hedgehog hair is far from fair,
But his eyes are dark like the midnight air.
His lips are pink like candyfloss and his legs are long and slim,
The boy who sits next door, I adore.
My knees quiver, as he shakes his head,
From the question that Miss just said.
The boy who sits next door, I adore.

He's been naughty, he's been sent to our class!
He grabs the chair next to me.
I feel my face turn funny, my legs shake,
It feels like there is an earthquake.
Then suddenly, *whoosh!*
Flies sick across the room
I feel like a right baboon.
He says, 'Err! I'm outta here!'
So he runs to the other room.
My mind turns blank, has he pulled a prank?
I just don't know to be frank!
The boy who sits next door, I adore.

Amy Gravelle (12)
Filton High School

Red Carpet

Walking along the red carpet,
Flashing cameras for the papers,
They've spent an hour in hair and make-up,
To get all glammed up.

Sitting in the crowd, waiting to see if they've won.
Performing songs, on the stage,
Getting nervous, practising their speech.

They've got the award,
They start their speech,
Crying, but not enough to smudge their make-up.

Signing autographs,
Walking back along the red carpet,
To get in their limos,
More pictures, for the papers.

Becky Cooke (12)
Filton High School

Cow

Chewing chewing all day long
Pooing pooing all day long
Friday is milking
Night-time is time for going to the shed
And the hay is my bed
In the morning the sun blinds my eye
And my child starts to cry
My child moves into a pen
I don't know why he's friends with a hen
I hate those sheep
When they start to bleet
It gets on my nerves
When I eat curds
And that's my day.

Danny Carlier (12)
Filton High School

Fruit

The fruit I like most is an orange or plum
They're sweet and they're juicy within
Of course I like oranges and plums oh I do
But there are others I like in the bowl.

Pears and apples, crunchy and soft
The taste goes down and refreshes your mouth
But you if they are too early or late they're sharp, a horrible taste
And yet, yes again there are more in my favour.

Water melons and melons themselves
The juice dribbling down my chin
Oh give me another, flesh without the skin
But there are two more I cannot resist.

Cherries and strawberries
Bite-size and cute
I can't wait to eat
My tasty fruit salad.

Kirsty Haslam (12)
Filton High School

The Dog

There was once a big white dog
He came in very tired
He saw a big green frog
Next to his owner who just got fired

He's standing by the sink
I think he wants a drink
He's laid back down after going to town
And now he's feeling down

His owner said, 'Come here
Tomorrow I'm diving deep
Don't worry there's nothing to fear
When you go fast asleep.'

Jodie Thomas (12)
Filton High School

Hungry And Homeless

I wake up in the morning,
With a stiff back,
Everyone staring at me,
As they walk past.

Everyone laughing and chatting,
All having fun
And me,
Just slumped in a doorway,
With a numb bum.

Nowhere to sleep,
Nothing to eat,
I can smell the delicious smell,
From the restaurant behind me.

Martine Pritchard (12)
Filton High School

Homeless

As I crouched on the hard, cold concrete of the city centre,
With frostbite beginning to spread over my body
Like ice-cold water running through my joints.
I'm slumped 24/7 imagining my fantasy,
A family, a house, a room,
My very own bouncy, comfortable bed.
All day long I can hear people chatting and laughing at me,
The smell of fast foods wafting past my red nose,
Also the scent of the rich aftershave or perfume
From the rich ones who turn their noses up at me.
As I shrivel in the doorway
I have the bitter taste of nicotine and alcohol
And I can almost taste the smell of chips that waves down the street.

Jade Daly (12)
Filton High School

My Homeless Poem

I live on the street,
I have nothing to eat,
I see the disgust in the eyes of others,
As I rise to my feet.

I see the children,
Running, giggling, having fun.
As the sun comes up
And my feet have gone numb.

I have pictures in my head,
Of a soft cosy bed,
Lots of money,
Warm clothes and food in my tummy.

I smell the chips from the chip shop
Down the road,
The bins, the sewers
And my smelly clothes.

Samantha Williams (12)
Filton High School

A Tramp's Sad Life!

The poor, poor man why are people so mean?
It's not his fault he's not very clean
He has no one to love him or say that they care
He has no food or clean clothes to wear
He sleeps on a seat or bench in the park
He is alone with his thoughts and dreams in the dark
When will he have a nice warm bed?
How sad these thoughts that go on in his head
One by one he watches his friends disappear
At last the police stopped, the man committed the crime
Perhaps it will now get better with time.

Lauren Hucker (12)
Filton High School

Street Wars

The life of the homeless
Not a pretty sight
You sleep on the freezing cold concrete
What a life
My fingers like icicles
And my body is tight.

The smell of burgers and chips
Makes me dribble all down my lips
The taste of rubbish is disgusting and minging.

I see people with money
I ask
They say no
Not even a penny they drop down below
They look at us like we are scum
But what have we done?

What I imagine is not likely to come
I dream of a bed
And even a roof over my head
But I might as well forget it
'Cause it's not true
Just me and my concrete floor
Will do.

Josh Wiltshire (12)
Filton High School

Untitled

As I turned round, I saw this chip in the wall.
It was below this board that was a picture of a sword,
As I focused on the chip in the wall.

It was strange, it was deep
And it looked like a sheep,
As I had a quick peep at the wall.

George Copas (12)
Filton High School

Love

My love doesn't know,
Like a fire my desire burns,
My love doesn't know,
How like a plant my love for her glows.

Like a star she shines,
In the vast, empty space above,
Her eyes twinkle and blink
And her mouth smiles and frowns.

Her hair, so fine, her face so pretty,
She is a princess, without the snob,
She is a flower whose beauty grows,
How like a planet my love for her glows.

But she is an angel, fallen from Heaven,
She shines up my day,
She takes sunshine and sky
When she goes.

I know my chances are a million to one,
I know her prince will come,
I know that my chances are slim,
How my love for her glows like a planet.

Compared to her, Mother Nature is pollution,
Compared to God, she is just Amen,
Fragile and kind, let her dark hair unwind,
Such beauty from above, she is my love.

Sam Scott (13)
Filton High School

The Sun

The sun is round as a pound,
It is yellow, like the flowers in the meadow.
The sun is bright like night,
It is bigger than a massive digger.

Charmaine Newland (12)
Filton High School

I Love That Murderer

Tonight was a cold night,
The wind was blowing with anger.

She held her hat so it would not fall off,
She came towards her house and opened the door in a rush,
Then she slammed it shut.

She knelt by the fire and took off her scarf, shoes and hat,
Then took a seat and relaxed.

Then suddenly the door knocked and she jumped in fright.
She glided to the door and opened it.
Then she saw a tall, handsome man.
She fell in love with him and offered him a seat and some tea.

As she was making the tea, the handsome man rose from his seat,
Then drew his knife and hid behind the kitchen door.

As Clair came through the door,
The handsome man stabbed her five times.
He then took all her money and left.

Then Clair was dead on the floor,
With blood all over the place.

Mitchell Ranklin (13)
Filton High School

Clocks

It ticks, its hands drawing time ever closer
Moving the hand towards a number
The protective plastic layer stops dirt
Time is quick, but sometimes slow.

Mainly two colours, black and white
But one stands out all alone
The second hand is red
It is the quickest, quicker than any other.

Matthew Harper (12)
Filton High School

The Pencil Case

I stare at the dark black rectangle
With one eye and a mouth laughing at me.
I see a red strip of blood in his mouth just lying there,
Waiting for something to happen.

Its mouth zips shut, but then a bigger one opens.
I see a load of helpless pens screaming, 'Help, help!'
Its mouth shuts once again,
Then the black rectangle falls into my bag,
Then I hear, 'Who's the bully now?'

'Help! Help!' it cries,
But no one can hear.
The bag said, 'Let the pens go you bully,
Or you will stay in me forever.'
'I'm sorry bag, I didn't mean it. I'll be good.
Please let me see the light again.'

George Miller (12)
Filton High School

Woman Beater

I cry so much it feels like rain
only because he's beat me again.

Last night I only ordered a pasty
and he got really nasty.

I looked a disgrace
then he shoved roses in my face.

I got fed up, I gave him a bash
then a smash - the neighbours heard a crash.

I realised what I had done,
I wish I could just run and run.

Kimberley Watkins (12)
Filton High School

Puppet Girl

She chose to walk alone
No one wondered why
Like a puppet on string
Wishing she would die

She pitied every blade of grass
Hoping it would stay
Working even harder
Struggling for each day

She waited so long
Until an autumn day
Spread her wings and then was gone
And not a word had stayed

The trees did not witness
The sky refused to tell
But no one in this world
Ever wondered why
The lonely girl on puppet strings
Wished she would forever die.

Charlotte Lovell (13)
Filton High School

Supersonic Flying Mouse

Supersonic flying mouse
Soars over skyscrapers
And reads newspapers
He eats roasted chestnuts
And hoggywestnuts
The wind blows in his face
He always carried a strawberry lace
The supersonic flying mouse.

Sam Thomas (12)
Filton High School

Streetwise

There was a young man who lived on the street
Who would walk around town
With cold and damp feet

He would walk around for days
Trying to get some cash
But people didn't bother
And just walked right on past

He thought he was forgotten
Battered and bruised
So every night he would
Push his head down public loos

There was a young man who lived on the street
Who one day got knifed
Whilst standing on his feet.

Harry Cheesley (12)
Filton High School

Covering Curtains

Curtains swaying through the air
Flying freely, rippling side to side
Rough and dark the fabric is
Wrinkled and mangled
So dark, not letting sunlight through
Hanging so long in the wind
Wide and big, stretching along the walls
Covering the sun's rays
Ripples like the tide
Behind the black lies.

Luke Webster (12)
Filton High School

Wings

I want to fly,
I want to be a bird,
I want to feel the wind race under my wings,
To soar through the air like a bullet,
To drift on warm thermals,
To skim over a lake picking off small flies,
I want to float on silent wings
Like an owl in the night,
I want to race like a falcon,
Hover over my prey,
My eagle eyes scanning the ground,
I want to paddle upstream, a swan,
And shake my broad wings,
Like a gannet, pierce the cool oceans like a dart,
I want to see the world with a real bird's eye view
And tuck my head under my wing and drift into a feathered dream,
As I sit and write this,
Watching, gazing at the seagulls gliding so high,
I slip away with my imagination,
Where I feel the wind under my wings
And look at the world below me
And touch the sun-blessed sky.

Emily Challis (13)
Filton High School

Autumn

Leaves falling off the tree
People hurry to get in
Fog everywhere I look
People going early
Time for me to go in before I get a cold.

Luke Smart (12)
Filton High School

My Love

When I first met him,
I thought he was the one,
Until I saw him with his girlfriend,
She wasn't pretty, she was dumb.

My lover sits across the room,
I stare at him from my seat.
Spiked up hair, dark blue eyes
And a face that you could eat.

He is my Romeo,
I want to be his Juliet.
I'd kiss him and kiss him,
Without regret.

His personality is great
And he is really clever,
My feelings for him are strong,
I will love him forever and ever.

I'd love to run away with him,
Or sail across the sea.
I'd row to a faraway island,
Where he is all mine, and forever we will be.

Hayley Ruderham (13)
Filton High School

Autumn

Foggy mornings darker nights
Smoky breath what a sight
Squirrels up and down the trees
Tumble down golden leaves.
Warm jumpers to keep me warm
Dewdrops nicely formed.

Steve Martin (13)
Filton High School

Who Am I? Can You Guess?

Who am I? Can you guess?
The snow,
A big, white carpet surrounds me
As I walk across it.

I lie on my back,
I feel the bitterly cold,
Freezing, stone-cold ice,
I shiver.

I smell a sea lion
Eating the last scraps of fish
On the side of the water.

I see a strange thing
Dawdling towards me,
A fat, flappy thing.
I'm starving.
                    Snap!

Jake Black (12)
Filton High School

Chairs

Bent, bendy plastic
Youth sits
Works
Fidgets
Body warmth heats it up
It stands, still and silent.

Bubbly texture
On your legs
Earth-coloured legs
End of the day you will know
On the table they will go.

Hannah Leworthy (13)
Filton High School

You Don't Know What It's Like To Be Homeless

You don't know what it's like to be homeless,
Watching people eating and throwing away food that they can't eat.
You don't know what it's like to be homeless,
Seeing children turning their light off and going to sleep in their
lush, warm beds.

You don't know what it's like to be homeless,
Staring at happy people who've just done their shopping with bags
full of outstanding food.
It's like having a knife stabbing you constantly.
You don't know what it's like to be homeless,
The angry wind forcing you to freeze.

You don't know what it's like to be homeless,
The frozen concrete biting away at you.
You don't know what it's like to be homeless, do you?

Lee Browne (13)
Filton High School

My Murderous Mixture

A rat's tail
And the shell of a snail,
Nose of a dog
And green mud from a bog.
Mix together and then put
A litre of sweat from your own foot,
Hear it bubble, see it spit
Add in an old gym kit.
Chop up a cow's udder
It will make you shudder,
Add it carefully
And put in a mouldy pea.
A dead sheep's wool
To make it all cool,
And feed to the unsuspecting victim.

David Brown (12)
Filton High School

My True Love

When I first saw you,
I knew that I loved you,
When you first looked at me,
I felt myself go red.
Did you really like me,
Or was it in my head?
But now I know my love is true
And I really, really love you.

I love it when you look at me,
You make me crazy,
Let me tell you now,
You're extraordinary, baby.
You make me feel like dancing
And singing in the rain,
Ever since I saw you,
I've never felt the same.

I truly love you, I always will,
But we can never be together.
I sit glaring at you in your leather,
Hoping some day we'll be together.
You've lived by me,
Ever since I was a baby.
You used to hold me in your arms
And calm me with your charms.
But that was long ago
And probably never again, I know.

I truly love you, I always will,
But I used to hate it when,
You brought your girlfriends home
And kissed them by the door,
And that was enough to leave me crying on the floor.

I truly love you, I always have and I always will.

Rachel Hill (13)
Filton High School

What If?

What would you do
If you found you love fish?
I would have it for dinner
In a big, pink dish.

What would you do
If you found you hate meat?
I would squish it and squash it
With my big, smelly feet.

What would you do
If you found you love toys?
I would get them all
And chase all the boys.

What would you do
If you found you hate money?
I would laugh and laugh
And think you were funny.

What would you do
If you found you love blue?
I would wrap it up
And send it to you.

What would you do
If you found you hate frogs?
I would take them back
And get thousands of dogs.

What would you do
If you found you're in love?
I would feel like I am riding
On a big, white dove.

Amber Turner (12)
Filton High School

She Stands Alone

She stands alone
her soul laid bare
in a trance
a constant stare

She blinks but once
and sheds a tear
she cannot rest
for doubt and fear

They clasp her wrists
and chain her down
in self-hatred
she will drown

There is no freedom
hope or light
time consumes
and holds her tight

Trapped and empty
motionless, deep
crying for her heart
to keep

Still it seems
she is without
a single thing
to smile about

Though time will fly
and wounds will heal
none of what she feels
is real

One moment finds
another loss
no bridges has
she come across

Stuck firm and fading
rapidly
she longs so much
to only be

Part of this world
that truly spins
and in the end
she stands
          and wins.

Beth Wilson (13)
Filton High School

Death

Death is the darkness that creeps up on little kids,
When their parents turn off the light.
Lying there with the blankets pulled around their necks,
Hearing noises, creaking floorboards.
But at least they know, when they fall asleep,
They'll wake up again in the morning.

Death is a bore for teenagers,
Living life to the full, for the moment.
Not worrying, not caring,
Not needing to care.
Dreaming of crushes, dreaming of the future,
They'll wake up again in the morning.

For 40-year-olds, death is sorting their lives out for their kids,
'Who will look after them? And I want a nice funeral.'
Organising, planning, children looking at them like they're mad,
But telling themselves, 'It's for Annie' or whoever.
The only time they get peace is when they're in their bedroom.
Asleep, thinking of the time they went to the park or the zoo,
They'll wake up again in the morning.

Death is a release of OAPs,
With different worries, aches and pains.
Taking hundreds of tablets every year,
Trying to sort each other out, but never quite succeeding.
Curling up in their warm beds after the mountain climb up the stairs,
They know they could be better in the morning.

Stephanie Johnson (14)
Filton High School

Dead Soon

I haven't got long to live
Life is getting shorter now
I wish I had more time
To have fun again.
My grandchild by my side
And my kids help me through
Here I lay down on my bed
And hope I do not die
Without saying a big goodbye
To all my friends and family.
They say I'm going to live forever
But now I know I'm not.
I have this certain feeling
That someone is waiting for me
At the gates of Heaven
To come and collect my soul.
Things are going so quickly
I can't remember some things.
Like my grandchildren's names
My husband died a year ago
Now I am very lonely
I can't wait to go and see him
Up there in the beautiful skies
Where I will join him soon.

Lisa Davenport (13)
Filton High School

Cold, Wet Feet

I am sat in a doorway with cold, wet feet,
Sat 'ere wondering what's to eat,
Watching the passers-by struggle across to the next street,
They don't give a damn about my cold, wet feet,
They just want to leg it across to the next street!
. . . But face it, I am just a man with cold, wet feet and, nothing to eat.

Kerrieanne Stadon (13)
Filton High School

Murder In The Night

It was the middle of the night,
The wind was howling outside,
I heard a movement, it gave me a fright,
I reached into my bottom drawer
And pulled out my knife.
Dagger in my mouth I began to crawl,
I saw a shadow and froze.
I took the dagger out of my mouth,
Sprang up against the wall and was still.
I saw the shadow move, it was holding something sharp,
Dagger clenched in my fist,
Heart pumping, I leapt around the corner,
Hacking away at whatever was in my way.
The wind was roaring outside,
A sharp pain hit me in the chest
And then, *thud!* The body fell to the floor.
Frightened and worried, I turned on the light,
Dead on the floor was my little brother,
A pair of scissors fixed in his hand.
I cried, oh did I cry!

Gareth Plant (13)
Filton High School

He's Gone!

I went downstairs in the night,
I went downstairs with only one light,
I went downstairs, I saw something move,
My heart was beating really fast too,
I couldn't believe it, there was someone in the house,
I was moving as quietly as a mouse,
I went to hit him with a bat,
After all, it was only a rat.

Madhavi Panchal (12)
Filton High School

The Sun

The sun shone
through my window as I got out of my bed.

The sun shone
as I walked out my front door.

The sun shone
on the children as they played football in the park.

The sun shone
as I had a water fight with my nephews.

The sun shone
as I sat in my garden watching the fish in the pond.

The sun shone
as I walked in my front door.

The sun shone and shone
as it shone into the future.

Josh Sheppard (13)
Filton High School

Being Homeless

Imagine how it would be living on the streets,
Night after night,
Day after day,
Smelling the smell of the sewer,
Watching people eat their dinner,
Watching, waiting for people to chuck out their leftovers.
But that's how life is
For a homeless person living on the streets,
Night after night,
Day after day,
But hey, that's life.
Well, that's my life anyway
And I'm used to it,
So don't feel sorry for me,
I'll survive.

Georgina Denning (13)
Filton High School

Love

Love is a fact
It should be told
If you've got no love
Your blood must be cold.
There are people you like
And people you hate
But the one you love
Is truly great.

Love is a fact
And should be told
Do not tell love
When it is old.
Love is a fact
And should be told
Love is a fact
Love!

Frank Davis (13)
Filton High School

Don't Kiss In The Garden!

Don't kiss in the garden
Don't kiss at the gate
Because love is blind
But neighbours ain't!

Don't hold hands in the dark
Don't hold hands in the shade
Because love is blind
But children ain't!

Don't be in love
Don't make a mistake
Because love is blind
But the sun ain't!

Danielle Taylor (13)
Filton High School

Lady Macbeth

She stalks the castle passages,
her black eyes piercing the darkness,
her long black hair swarming around her shoulders,
her elegant stature, is not so elegant elsewhere.

Her web of deceit runs deep,
right from her heart,
filling others with despair.

She preys on her husband's free mind
and uses his ambition,
to fuel her own.

Nothing will stand in her way,
dagger, danger, death,
dagger, danger, death.

The eye of the storm
follows her, never leaving,
her desire never wavers,
but grows and grows and grows.

Gemma Goldsack (13)
Filton High School

Stupid Boy

Shut up, you stupid boy
Don't poke yourself in the eye!
Don't be such a stupid boy
Don't try and eat that tiny toy!

Don't hit the wall or chuck that ball
You stupid boy!
You're like a little five-year-old
Who just won't listen when he's told!

Why won't you just shut your mouth!

Nicole Lawrence (13)
Filton High School

My Ballad

Standing tall
all was well,
they didn't know
soon they'd be saying farewell.

Along came a plane
nobody knew,
high in the sky
the plane then flew.

One burst into flames
the other one stood tall,
people screaming
as the other people began to fall.

The last one standing
high in the sky,
people shouting and screaming
as they saw the plane high.

It began to fall
everybody knew,
this would be the last
of the Twin Towers,
as it burnt into two.

Katie Walsh (13)
Filton High School

Pencil And Paint

Winter has a pencil
For pictures clear and neat,
She traces the black treetops
Upon a snowy sheet.
But Autumn has a palette
And a painting brush instead,
And daubs the leaves for pleasure
With yellow, brown and red.

Riyadh Ahmed (13)
Filton High School

I Love You

His hair is not like any other,
it's smooth and soft and brown,
it shines in the day
and in the moonlight,
as he brushes it off his forehead.

He wears trendy clothes,
so he looks so fine,
his cologne is breathtaking,
it blows my mind.

I could go on forever,
talking 'bout him,
the way he walks
and the way he talks,
I just want to say,
I love him!

Rachel Barrington (13)
Filton High School

The War In Iraq

The war in Iraq I cannot explain
The people in Iraq are under terrible strain,

Once it was a peaceful place
Then came along the human disgrace,

He goes by the name of Saddam Hussein
And has caused many people horrible pain,

His son's football team once lost a game
So he shot them in the head and said,
'Oh what a shame.'

The families of the dead all they can do is grieve
Hoping that the UN forces will just get up and leave.

All you ever hear now is that more lives are lost
But Tony Blair knew this war would come at a cost.

Taylor King (13)
Filton High School

My Love

My love is over there
he looks marvellous
I am too shy to ask him out
even though I love him

The way he smiles
the way he winks
the way he walks
the way he talks

He makes me shake
he makes me quiver
he makes me shiver
he makes me feel faint

My love is over there
he smiles over at me
I go weak and can't smile
I go wobbly and faint.

Gemma Mitchell (13)
Filton High School

Macbeth Poem

Macbeth, a strong man
Who is as strong as a stampede of horses and men
Macbeth is sneaky and fast with his sword
At the end of the battle Macbeth sees three witches

They tell him what he did not know
Thane of Cordor he was going to be!
Banquo would have children for kings
But Macbeth would be king too if Duncan could be murdered

Macbeth couldn't grab the dagger
He thought he could see
But he used the one he had in his hand
To kill *his* king and take his place.

Timmy Wybrow (13)
Filton High School

Prehistoric Garden

When I get a house of my own
I will make my garden
I will fill it with primitive plants
Just like the age of the dinosaurs.

Walking one day in my garden
I go and sit by my pond
This is my special thinking place
Where I sit on my bench and ponder.

I close my eyes and drift away
I think of a world gone by
When I open my eyes my pond is a river
My garden an endless view.

By the riverbank in front of me
A lizard I think I saw
Upright and about the size of a dog
Not a lizard but a dinosaur!

It drinks at the riverbank
Looking around between sips.
It is a plant-eating hipsilophodon
From 120 million years ago.

From the forest beside the river
There comes a frightening roar
The little hipsilophodon runs away
I look at the forest and wait.

Out of the tree it comes
Much bigger than the hipsilophodon
A crocodile head and huge clawed hands
It is a meat-eating baronyx.

The baronyx stops by the river
It turns and looks at me
It slowly comes much closer
Until we are nose to nose.

Its eyes look into mine
It sniffs me suspiciously
It opens its mouth, I hold my breath
It roars like thunder.

I close my eyes with horror
The roaring noise stops
All around me is silence
Slowly I open my eyes.

My garden is back to normal
The river is again a pond
My bench is back in its place
It is my special thinking place again.

I sit back down on my bench
And looking at the pond
I notice there are footprints on the ground
Huge with three big toes.

Robert Graham (13)
Filton High School

You Are!

You are my Becks, I am your Posh,
You are my king, I am your queen.
My love for you is as sweet as candy,
You are my Danny, I am your Sandy.

I love the way you tell a joke,
I need you lots because you're my bloke.
The way you smell when you stroll past,
I inhale so much so it will last.

Your hair is so dark and brown,
Every time you're not in school, I feel so down.
You are my Romeo, I'm your Juliet,
We will never be together as long as time is set.

My love for you is like a rose,
I love the way you wear trendy clothes.
I even love the way you walk,
You really impress me when you talk.

Daniella King (13)
Filton High School

Lady Macbeth

A waterfall of black hair falls down her back
And a river of blood flows through her head,
As she thinks of her victim, so innocent, so weak,
Lying peacefully in his bed.

Her eyes pierce through the dark corridor
And a wicked smile gleams silently in the black,
She sighs as she thinks of her loved other half,
Who evilness lacks.

She slowly glides on and her red silk dress rustles,
As she comes to the entrance of the room of the soon to be no more.
She glances around and smiles with delight,
As she slowly pushes open the door . . .

The deed was done, the crown was won,
Without any hitches, a squeak or a groan.
Her heart beat fast as she washed the blood off her hands,
The heart that was made of stone.

Amy Hamlen (13)
Filton High School

Lady Macbeth

Her long black hair
Her skin so fair
Cats' eyes gleaming
They look so deceiving
That false, evil smile
So devious and vile
And all that she feels
Is the desire to kill.
The crimson silk from her dress
Reflects on her eyes
Her need to be Queen
Continues to rise.

Natasha Sheppard (13)
Filton High School

The Witches

The witches tell evil to the world,
They're always plotting, with evil on their side.
All they think about is evil prophecies and speech,
They love dragging people onto their own evil side.

Their arms are spindly branches,
Just broken from a tree.
Their hair is wispy iron wire
Grey and coarse.

They are unreal, not human,
Who vanish mysteriously, under your nose.
They predict the future to innocent souls,
Which provoke their minds to kill!

Macbeth was one innocent soul,
He was spooked out and killed,
The most important man in Scotland,
Because of selfishness and greed.

Clare Hepburn (13)
Filton High School

Lady Macbeth

She is as sly as a prowling puma looking for prey,
Her eyes are cats' eyes with daggers gleaming inside,
Her smile is like that of a wicked witch,
Her silky, long black hair is like a snake's.

She is as sly as a snake slithering away from guilt,
She has death on her mind like a demon,
She reeks of sweet success,
Her head is full of murder.

Blood, blood, blood
Her head is full of murder.

Emily Naish (13)
Filton High School

The Witch Of Darkness

Full of pure poison
She slithers sneakily around like a spooky snake
In other people's business.

Fiddly frail fingers
Her hair, straw and spaghetti-like
Snapping off in her horrid hand.

Sly as a serpent
She speaks of pathetic prophecies
Involving innocent souls.

Her bony, bent over body
Scuttling around like a scorpion
Shaking up everyone she sees.

A crooked smile
A ragged and rough-looking rat
Disappearing under the blanket of darkness.

Rachel Haines (13)
Filton High School

Life

I have a boyfriend
who I don't get to see!
Life is crap for
both him and me!
I can't ring him,
for I have no credit on my phone!
When he's not around I feel so alone!
I'm always grounded
and so is he!
Why has life,
gone wrong for me?

Anna Wilmot (13)
Filton High School

Not Anymore

The innocent flower but there's a serpent beneath
weak like a puppy yet a courageous lion
who defends his family and friends.
Walks like a tiger ready to pounce
his heart is of silver as he is not yet gold
his ears are deaf to danger.
A strong as an ox yet when shown the wrong things
can wither right down till there's nothing but heart.
Thoughtless yet calm, opens his arms to the evil
and dangerously walks sword with sword
with the devious and cunning
breaks bread, drinks wine with the sly and sneaky.
A bell starts to ring
the death of the King!
Not so kind anymore
no longer the puppy,
now he is wiser and stronger
and confused that he might be next to see the great light.

Kayleigh Smith (13)
Filton High School

Football Is Cool

Football, football, football is cool
You play it at home and you play it at school
Me and Kamal are the best two
But Sach and Jake are a load of poo!

You kick it
You trick it
You skill them out
But when they come to tackle you
You run the way out.

Chris Regan (13)
Filton High School

Manchester United V Arsenal

Man U V Arsenal what a game
The words, the abuse
It was like watching rugby
The game was going to be tight like an angle - obtuse.

Keane leads out the team
60,000 screaming fans
Arsenal players just being booed
Man U fans sat just sat drinking their cans.

Ferguson angry, kicking tin cans
Arsenal cheating as always
Nistelrooy tackled, Viera kicks then sent off
Nistelrooy shouts to ref.

Forlan is taken down
Penalty said the ref
Nistelrooy hits the bar
Keown hits him, what a clown.

Manchester United V Arsenal, 0-0
What a game, both teams drown in sorrow
United will beat them again tomorrow.

Charlie Warrington (13)
Filton High School

A Day In The Life Of A Gangster

Come on people what can we do?
We fight, we kill and hang out with our crew,
Punching people it's da best,
It beats crying, it's better than the rest.
Now people say we always fight,
I fight all day, I fight all night,
But I don't care what they say,
It's my thing, it's my way.

Kamal Ahmed (13)
Filton High School

Meeting With A Witch

An evil, twisted smile will greet you,
Flashing evil, gleaming fangs from a wolf,
Dripping with the blood of a fresh kill,
But don't look to her eyes,
They are black, solid cats,
That will burn through you
With the heat of a white-hot fire
And make horrid images appear in your head
That unfixes your hair.
You want to break free but you can't
You're trapped
You see her snake-like hair,
Sliding and slithering over her head.
Creeping silently around you like a hunting tiger
Ready to strike.
You hear a husky, fog-like voice telling you a future
But don't believe it's good.
Horrible things could lie ahead,
You try and speak
You hear a pop
And next thing you know,
You are on your own again,
On your own.

Michaela Mill (13)
Filton High School

Macbeth

His hair is like Spaghetti Junction on the motorway,
His mind is a tornado about to break away.

He is good on the inside but gets put off sometimes,
His wife doesn't help, her words explode like landmines.

He'll live in guilt forever,
He killed Duncan the best king in Scotland ever.

Miles Lewton (13)
Filton High School

Life's Not Fair

I hate my life
It's just not fair
My parents won't let me go anywhere.

My mum's embarrassing
My dad's the same
When they talk to my friends
I go insane.

'Where are you going?
What did you do?'
That's all they say
'And remember to tie up your shoe.'

When I'm out
When they're not around
My mum rings up,
'Come home at 8.30.'

Why do they do this?
I shouldn't care
But one thing's for certain
My life's not fair.

Callum Knapp (13)
Filton High School

Macbeth

Macbeth is as strong as a rampaging rhino
Macbeth is as loyal as a dog to his master
Macbeth is as brave as a knight in shining armour
Macbeth is as gentle as a flower blowing in the breeze
Macbeth is as evil as cats' eyes gleaming in the dark
Macbeth is a murderer.

Scott Davenport (13)
Filton High School

Stray

I'm a dog in a basket,
Sitting there
Come see me
And stroke my hair.

I'm a dog in a basket,
All alone
Come feed me
And give me a home.

I'm a dog in a basket,
Feeling sick
Come help me
This is no trick.

I was a dog in a basket,
All on my own
No one helped me
All I wanted was a home.

I was a dog in a basket,
Dreaming of a home
But no one cared for me
You all left me alone.

Sahara Chowdhury (13)
Filton High School

Winter Alder

Late October, giving heavy snow and hail
For 40 days I suffered with nature
At first just frost, and now my green blades begin to moult
Among others, we struggled and fell like autumn leaves
One by one.

Andrew Sperring (15)
Filton High School

Isabelle

The weather is changing all the time
The news explaining that everything should be fine
Homes and buildings getting wrecked every day
People hoping that twister Isabelle would fade away

Only a few seconds have passed
Where Isabelle stood spinning so fast
People looking for a place to hide
Not realising that other people have died

People standing outside to have a look
But off they went because they were took
Up in the air round and round
Before they knew it they were back on the ground

Rains and winds have passed right by
Leaving the wonderful blue sky
All that was left was rubbish, bits and bobs
Which had no use or any jobs

Homes and buildings were left in a horrible state
It's like the city was its bait
Now that Isabelle has gone we say goodbye
And are happy that we didn't die.

Gene Jozefowicz (13)
Filton High School

The Whiteboard

It stays in its place, day and night,
Dim with the times of use.
But still, it reflects the lights above,
In its attempt to stay in care.
It has grey patches where the marker doesn't come off,
Only a single sentence is written and that is:
Use your eyes to create poetry.

Naomi Bradley (13)
Filton High School

A Dream

There's a special someone in my dreams
I just can't figure out who it is,
It might be the boy down the road,
Or my mum or maybe even my friend Liz.
I want to know badly, all I can see is a shadow,
Never can see the face.
Can't see anything now, oh wait it's just come back
Still can't recognise a single thing, from head to base.
It's getting more interesting now, it's getting clearer,
Still can't figure out who it is,
Maybe it's got a bit more blurry.
Something's coming clear now,
It seems like a funny type of hair,
Who wants hair like that,
Especially with a head that looks like a pear.
It all is coming clear now,
I wonder what I see,
Oh my God you won't believe who it is,
It had to go and be *me!*

Francesca Carless (13)
Filton High School

The Oak Tree

That precious oak tree
Where we carved our names
To stand there, solid in the ground
For love, not ridicule, nor shame.

The summer that you spent by my side
Love an unchained melody
Untouched by the world
Seen by only you and me!

But, you found I wasn't that special one
Like the way I feel about you
You stole my heart I'm empty now
But I doubt you feel the same way too.

Holly Gilbert (13)
Filton High School

Arsenal Vs Manchester United

They've just kicked off
And the chants have begun.
The players on the pitch,
Directly under the sun.

The first half comes to an end,
Sadly for the fans there was no action.
The crowds await the second half,
Hoping for satisfaction.

Later on the whistle blows,
Viera had received a yellow card.
He must calm down,
Which he knew would be hard.

Two minutes later,
Another foul to commit.
Viera lashes out,
Hoping to hit.

The referee reaches into his pocket,
Pulls out the red card
And Viera is gone.

Joseph Tanner (13)
Filton High School

Fly Away

I wish I was a parrot
I want to fly away
I wish I was a parrot
Fly away and go on holiday
You should see all my colours on my wing
And my voice that sings

I want to be free
And live in a tree
In a nest
That's here it's best.

Kirsty Porter (13)
Filton High School

I Hate School

I hate school, it drives me up the wall
I can't believe I have to go to school,
But my mum tells me I have to.

I hate school, it drives me up the wall
Oh why do I have to go to school
And see people eating in the hall?

I hate school it drives me up the wall
Oh why do I have to go to school,
Can't I have home school?

School is so boring, school is just sad
School is boring, where everyone's bad
It's just making me mad.

Oh why do I have to go to school
Because what will I do for a job?

Amanda Harris (13)
Filton High School

Shoes

At the mall trying to choose
Looking for only one pair of shoes
I've got Nike, Adidas and Umbro too
Colours range from red to blue.
Shops from JD to JJB
It feels so great, choice is so free.

Looking in shops shouldn't take too long
I know what I want when it comes to shoes
I'm never wrong.
Money's no object I wanna look good
Wanna look how a real girl should.

I've bought them now a real nice pair,
They even match with my blonde hair.
I'm now ready to face the world
With my new shoes I'm a whole new girl.

Kelly Stinchcombe (13)
Filton High School

Annoying Babies

Babies are annoying
Babies are bad
Babies are smelly
And they get sad

They never listen
Just always cry
Sometimes I just wish
They would die

Tears from their eyes
Snot from their noses
Spit from their mouths
And I just shout

But they're alright
They finally sleep
Although I get paid
It's alright for me!

Jayna Panchal (13)
Filton High School

What I Want

I want Bentleys and roses and champagne galore,
Chocolate in boxes, brought straight to my door,
A Roman mosiac, piece by piece for my floor,
England to China, around the world tour?

I want palaces, kingdoms fit for a queen,
The biggest darn castle that was ever seen,
I'll ring up the President, 'Stop for some tea,'
All of my subjects would bow down to me!

I want woodland, forests and great rivers too,
Strong noble warriors who would always be true,
My two favourite colours - crimson and blue,
But just know this now, I'll give it all up for you.

Joe Smith (14)
Filton High School

When The Curtains Close

They're blue, they're big
They block out all the light
Makes the room so dark
So the lights come on and light it up

Then when they open
No need for lights
The sun pours in
Fills the room with light

All so light
All so bright
No need to fight
'Cause nothing is so bright
Nothing so powerful
Cannot be broken till the curtains shut

The big blue curtains begin to close
The light stops pouring in
No, please don't close!
They finally meet then the room is black
Black as a pitch-black night
All so black now I cannot see.

Mark Cornish (13)
Filton High School

My Eyes

Almond-shaped eyes sparkle
Out of painted shells black and blue

Long eyelashes curled and coloured
Black lines surround the almond

Green like the leaves on the tree
White and blue like the sky

Reflecting on the world around me.

Emily Williams (13)
Filton High School

The Storm

The storm was brewing out at sea
And was coming closer to you and me
The thunder clapped, the lightning struck
And flew away the gull and duck
The storm came closer and all took shelter
The tramp was running as the rain did pelt her
The wind was blowing the sand all around
A man's hat blew off and was never found
Lightning struck the town hall
The wind so strong made the trees fall
The storm was calming, the end was near
But still there was a sense of fear.
The clouds were shrinking
The light did grow
Then came back all the birds that did go.
The storm was over and all was silent
And all would remember the storm so violent.

Michael Weston (13)
Filton High School

My Body

My ears are rough
My head is tough

My arms are hairy
My face is scary

My shoulders are wide
They move from side to side

My legs are strong
My nose is long

Now I have to stop
Talking about my body

I will see you next time
Sorry.

Dan Lewis (13)
Filton High School

The Lion

The lion is crouching in the grass
Preparing to chase the speedy mass
The antelope is unaware
Of the beast that's waiting there.

The lion is ready, waiting to go
The antelope wandering to and fro.
Then he pounces, starting the chase,
The antelope running at high pace.

The race is on,
It's a race for life
The lion is giving
The antelope strife.

Then it's over
The antelope's dead
It gives up the struggle
And lays down its head.

Rebecca Nicholls (13)
Filton High School

Lady Macbeth

Cats' eyes, snake hair
Nothing else can compare
Red dress, what a mess
She can be nothing less.

Hunting walk,
Nails white as chalk,
She shouts with a squawk
She watches like a hawk.

She's made of stone
All alone
Her heart is a boulder
Could she be any colder?

Abbey Huelin (14)
Filton High School

Typhus

He stood straight and upright
The smoke drifted silently on
His body encased in armour
Spikes covered him

Shades of green and black
Were all that coloured him
Runes and faces all engraved
The skulls of his enemies impaled

His pain contorted features
Old and withered with time
Nothing would stand against him
Terror was his ally

His scythe crackled before him
It seeped the blood of men
It seeped the venom of snakes unknown
Souls bound within it called
Called for the blood of his enemies

He had once been faithful
He had once been typhoon
But now he'd changed
His anger now controlled him

Revenge he seeked
Against his once loyal friends
He longed for their deaths
He now was *Typhus*.

Steven Rugman (13)
Filton High School

Lady Macbeth

Pretty like butterflies fluttering through a summer's breeze
But poisonous like a snake, waiting to ambush prey.
Smart like an owl, ready to escape, but always ready to attack.
A heart of coal burning with fiery desire to be queen.

Kye Simpson (13)
Filton High School

My Poem On Conkers

October is the time for conkers,
It is when kids go bonkers.
Conkers are from the chestnut tree,
Which is just fine for you and me.

Conkers are a fun piece of nature,
The spiky shell opens when it is mature.
Children play with them across the land,
With the majestic nut in hand.

With conkers on a piece of string,
They battle until one goes ping.
The winner feels very glad,
The loser feels very sad.

If a conker is picked up rotten,
It is dropped and then forgotten.
The squirrel thinks it's the best,
The squirrel then takes it to the nest.

Unfortunately the season ends,
The kids only just talk to friends.
The kids always remember,
That the season comes again in October.

Peter Wakefield (13)
Filton High School

The Wall

The wall is silent and dirty,
It has no feelings at all,
The wall is bashed with chairs,
It doesn't shout when you bash it,
It can't scream, it can't do anything,
The wall just stands there,
Till it is bashed down,
It doesn't move, shift or anything.
It's a sad, lonely, nothing.

Kate Rennolds (13)
Filton High School

The Hundred Acre Wood

Come with me, come with me now to a special place,
an enchanted place, a place where Christopher Robin plays all day.
An enchanted wood filled with fun and games,
filled with tall oak trees, evergreens
and fine beech trees with lots of luscious, glossy green.
In this enchanted wood, Christopher Robin plays
by a river on a bridge,
having adventures all day long, adventures with all his friends.
Here is a donkey by the name of Eeyore, stuffed with sawdust,
glum by nature and always losing his tail.
Sitting in a tree proud and grand, there's Owl.
Along comes another one of Christopher Robin's friends,
small and timid but brave when needed, there's Piglet.
Here we have Rabbit, very organised and self-confident
and perhaps just a little arrogant,
along with him are Kanga and little Roo, a mother and child.
And here's Tigger, bouncy and brash and always full of fun.
Last but certainly not least, here comes the most important friend of all,
Winnie the Pooh, cuddly and tubby
and stuffed with fluff and guzzling honey,
to which Christopher Robin hugs him and says affectionately,
'Silly old bear.'

Welcome to the Hundred Acre Wood.

Carolyn Percy (13)
Filton High School

The Black Hole

Crawling up the ladder
Into her little house
Moving as an elephant
Squeaking like a mouse.

Curled up in the corner
Taking her last breath
Shivering in the cold
Leading to her death.

Samantha Waterhouse (15)
Filton High School

Time To Say Goodbye

It's time to say goodbye;
It's time to let go
To the memories we had
And the memories we know.

There is no one left to watch your steps;
No one to hold your hand
You find yourself slipping further
As you're left in lonely land.

The candle has burnt out
The tide is sweeping in
Your youthful skies are grey
And a new world now begins.

Your future is happening now
And things will never be the same
So now it no longer matters
Who it is to blame.

So say goodbye to everyone
And leave nobody out
You may regret it later
Your wake-up call is now.

Laina Fudgell (16)
Filton High School

Getting Old

Here I am old and grey
Sat here with my thoughts all day
Thinking about when I was young
How those days were filled with fun
Slowly my life is slipping away
Every night I sit and pray
Please let me stay I'm not done
I'm not ready to leave my grandson
He's too young to understand
I will move to a better land.

Nicole Scrase (13)
Filton High School

Twin Towers

The anniversary of the day has been
People grieving for their loved ones
It's hard to say if they can handle it
You could see the fire of a thousand suns.

Tears of sadness, none of joy
People rushing to the scene
Everyone speechless, time stood still
No one can believe the horror that's been.

Soldiers fighting for people's lives
Something happened, everything still
People watching trying to help
Everyone wishing to kill.

Everything choking by the smoke
Nothing to see, nothing you can do
To stop the grieving of loved ones
Who was responsible . . . who?

Leanne Stiddard (14)
Filton High School

Something About You

There's something about you
That I can't place
There's something about you
I see it in your face
There's something about you
As I gaze in your eyes
There's something about you
Like a birthday surprise
There's something about you
I think of you day and night
There's something about you
That I really like.

Emma Stadon (14)
Filton High School

My Love

Your clothes are smart,
Your hair is fine,
Oh how I wish
That you'd be mine.

Not being with you
Would make my heart go weak,
Cos you're the one
That sweeps me off my feet.

When I look at the stars
I wonder if you're looking too,
They always seem to get brighter
When I'm thinking of you.

My heart beats fast
When I see you,
Do you feel
The same way too?

Love can do
Such strange things,
Shivery feelings
And wedding rings.

Jess Warren (14)
Filton High School

Michael Owen

Michael Owen, young sensation,
With his goals he stuns the nation,
He runs so fast, he loves to shoot,
I think he'll win the golden boot,
With him and Kewell in the team,
Success is real, not just a dream.

Ollie Ahmed (14)
Filton High School

The Witches

Hunched back and a crooked nose
doing devil's work where no one goes.

A wicked smile,
a crippled face,
they look nothing like the human race.

Chanting and casting spells,
controlling others to doom.

A wicked smile,
a crippled face,
they look nothing like the human race.

Hooded and cloaked,
short and stumpy,
old and mad,
mean and grumpy.

Matthew Maddocks (14)
Filton High School

My Flats

Church view flats are the best
They're better than all the rest
The football goes bang, crash against the garages
The caretakers shouts, 'Get out the park!'
But we don't listen to her
The cats out there purr
We kick the little children about
Because they like to shout
Church view flats are the best flats
Listen it's true, it's true.

Gavin Seymour (14)
Filton High School

Lady Macbeth

Her long, black, snaky hair
Lies softly down her back
Her wicked smile shows her teeth
Like sharp, shiny daggers
Her eyes like cats'
Evil, dark and creepy
Her thoughts are about killing
And only killing
'When I am Queen,' she says
Sneaky and sly
She always wants power, power, power
To persuade Macbeth to kill, kill, kill
Duncan
She waves around devious and sly
She is good on the outside
But inside her soul is as dark as Hell
She tries to poison minds and think bad thoughts
She is Lady Macbeth sly and *deadly.*

Brooke Packwood (13)
Filton High School

Lady Macbeth

She has long hair like the black fur of cats
Her heart is like coal in the dark
She has milky blood of a guilty conscience
She is like a cave in the dark
She has a wicked smile like a witch in the dark
Devious mind like a wicked witch in the dark
She has daggers in her eyes of killing
She has spirits in her ears
She is as weak as snails.

Victoria Spiller (14)
Filton High School

War Is Laborious

War is laborious,
Not glorious,
As it's made out to be,
The smell is a stench
And would make you wretch.

People die
In the sky,
Underground,
On the ground,
And in the sea,
People don't dance
Around in glee.

No one wins,
They all crash,
And need to recover,
The economy slump,
Our planet look like a dump.

Just because one man,
One single man,
Wanted more power,
Or to shower,
In money and gold.

For war is laborious,
And not glorious,
As it's made out to be.

Sam Barnard (14)
Marlwood School

Do You . . .

Do you know what it's like
To be scared of your own shadow?
Living in a world of despair
Where all you see is hate?

Do you believe in angels?
Are they watching over us?
Protectors of our mortal lives
Guards sent down from above?

Do you know true happiness?
Have you felt the surging warmth
The feeling that everything's
Finally right, not out of place?

Do you know about perfection?
Is it something you would like?
Will it destroy the world
Or make us strive for danger?

Do you know the feeling
When you just don't belong on Earth?
Your presence is useless to them
And you want to collapse again?

Do you know what it's like to die
And fall away so lifelessly?
I don't know about you, but I do
Because I'm dying inside.

Jenny Clark (14)
Marlwood School

The Boy

He sits there in the corner
The sun shining through his golden hair
On the surface he is calm, underneath he is a mourner
He has been through his share.

His smile is kind, but hidden,
He can't do anything wrong,
Like wrong has been forbidden,
So he just sits there, getting on.

His parents, they know nothing,
They just think he's worthless,
To them he is not a human being,
Just a punch bag not at its best.

He has bruises all up his back,
Blue and green they are,
A fine punch his parents pack,
And they leave a mental scar.

He should be taken away,
But leave he cannot,
They will kill him someday,
And he'll be left to rot.

Mary Bartlett (14)
Marlwood School

Undercover In The Back Alley World

Dark
Dangerous
A sinister underworld
Dank
Dingy
Bad and bent
Dodgy
Deserted
Concise crime
Disastrous
Disciplined
Death at the hands of the hoods

It's a dangerous world out there
Watch your step
Turn the wrong way
And that's it

You're in too deep
No way out
Trouble
The problems with organised crime.

Aaron Cottrell (14)
Marlwood School

Another Way?

I've always been taught
That two wrongs don't make a right
And you can't solve anything in a fight.

But now all that seems forgotten
Reason lost in anger
No one sees what's happening.

Killing more won't bring them back
It won't make it easier
It won't make the pain go away.

I'm not forgiving what they did
Because that will never happen
But think how many people will never forgive us.

I see the hunger
The houses destroyed
Who's causing the terror in their eyes?

Revenging the death of innocent people
By killing more
Isn't there another way?

Causing pain, hunger, suffering
Destroying, killing, hurt
Isn't there another way?

Katherine Hirst (15)
Marlwood School

A King's Psalm

I drink in this life from cups of silver
and eat from bowls of gold,
but I'd prefer the life of a London pauper,
his memory lost and story ne'er told.
For I have all I want, it's true,
but I am lacking what I need,
nothing of matter, no drink, no food,
can end this want, saviour to me.
I *could* say love would save this curse,
but I have never sampled the taste,
I promised myself, for better or worse,
I *would not* let this life go to waste,
but show the world my talent is true,
shout it to the end of all time,
sing of the days when the skies are blue,
and times when the dream was mine.
For I drink in this life from cups of silver
and eat from bowls of gold,
but the day I can take my talent further,
my memory is found and my story told.

James Bunting (14)
Marlwood School

Stones Carved Out Of Wood

The starting line draws nearer
Firing shots leap forward
Men lying face down in mud
as women dream of being reunited

Balancing on barbed wire
Bodies hung with dignity
Lives lost at war
as women were fed up of the wait

Mothering views of trench life
Blind young boys sign up
Slaughtered like ants
Their mothers wait for news

The Hun were just young men
Blindfolded by racist views
as they helped to murder
women and children together.

Alice Oldfield (14)
Marlwood School

Racoon

He is known as El Bandito
And slinks here and there,
He sticks to the shadows
Sending dustbins flying everywhere.

This comic James Bond
Is tricky and masked,
The police never catch him
Because he's clever and fast.

This swift little creature
Is a pain in the neck,
He never stops stealing
Because he's a wreck.

Sam Gardner (12)
The Castle School

Up, Up And Away!

This day we fly high to France,
Yellow signs calling for our luggage,
It disappears through a flap like a lion eating its lunch,
Big, small, square, round, guitars and skis into the black hole,
Through the crime checks and flashing lights,
The lasers searching like eagles' eyes,
Kitted with guns, the policemen stand proud and tall,
Loud, calling announcement ringing through your ears.

Onto the plane one by one,
Passports scanned by guards like eagles searching for mice,
Rows of three, rows of two,
Where's my chair?
Seat belts fastened, arm rests down,
Demonstrations for safety, pulling my eyes to them,
Gaining speed, louder noises,
Out the window everything seems further away,
Clunk, a shake, wheels in, we're up,
Like an arrow shooting into the air.

Up, up and away,
Soaring through the air like a bird,
My eyes flash green as I stare out the window
overlooking green carpets,
We float over the world,
Like a teacher over his children,
Surrounded by cotton wool we bounce and glide through
the bowl of water.

Ears pop as the plane drops,
Rushing down through the clouds like we are late for work,
Visions gradually getting larger as we lower in the air,
Children cry from pain and fright,
The airport in sight, what a relief,
Wheels popping out pulling the plane down,
Bump, there is an elephant falling from the sky,
Zooming down the runway, we can't stop,
Transforming from a hare to a tortoise we eventually pull to a halt,
We are here at last but the journey must be made again next week.

Amy Derham (12)
The Castle School

Through That Door

Through that door
is a graveyard
horrifying to all
with gates forever barred.

Where it's always dark
and the ghosts rule
you wouldn't survive
for they are so cruel!

Through that door
is a never-ending fight
between good and evil
it's a terrible sight.

Where bodies form the carpet
and everywhere is gone
the noise was deafening
I didn't like it here in this never-ending war.

Through that door
is a magical fairy-tale land
where the trees are chocolate
and there's always a band.

Playing all night
to the mythical creatures
whose hair was polka dot
and their gruesome features.

Through that door
is a magnificent ocean
with millions of fish
moving in one swift motion.

The vast turquoise waters
were full of beautiful sights
they held many tropical colours
from blacks to whites.

Through that door
is a millionaire's mansion
where family portraits hang from the walls
the enormous corridors headed in every direction.

Where everything is gold
the ceilings, floors and walls
where the cutlery is diamond
and they have three swimming pools.

Ben Sprackman (12)
The Castle School

My Journey

Onto the ship with its tall masts and swinging booms,
Into the indigo ocean up and down, up and down,
Through the white sands and husky palm and coconut trees,
Over the bulky sand dunes with their dinky islands of grass,
Onto the slinky hammock, slung between two bent trees,
Into the water and through the coral reef,
With its colourful testicle-like plants,
  Over the Maui islands, flying through the blue atmosphere.

Onto the soft, white blanket of snow,
Into the cold emptiness,
Through the freezing, terrifying snowstorm,
Over cracking opaque ice,
Onto the crackling fire goes my damp, frozen clothes,
Into the forest of green pine trees,
Through caves with hibernating grizzly bears!
  Over the dazzling white island of Greenland,

Onto the pebble beach,
Into the grey city of tall brown buildings,
Through the windy streets,
Over the blue wiry river bridge,
Onto the rainy fields,
Into the deserted country pub,
Through many long, sodden dirt tracks!
Over the grey-green island of England,
  Over the vast ocean, but where to now?

Grace Salvage (11)
The Castle School

Here In, Out Too And Into Poem

Here in England the cold wind blows,
Here in England horses are galloping and galloping,
Here in England screams of people shopping crazy,
Here in England cars are racing, cars are hooting,
Here in England smoke rises, in lunges, then dead.

Out to Italy the blood sun sets over the land,
Out to Italy the beach pattered with lizard prints,
Out to Italy the smell of warming pasta breathes in the air,
Out to Italy women shouting, 'Mama mia!'
Out to Italy the Leaning Tower of Pisa is falling, falling, falling down,
gone, not here.

Into Tobago the sea is blue and calm,
Into Tobago the pelicans are fishing,
Into Tobago the baking hot sun is rising,
Into Tobago the black-red hot sand burns till your feet hurt,
Into Tobago big coconuts come down like cannonballs.

Victoria Thompson (12)
The Castle School

Through That Door

Through that door
Is a field with a fence,
The pine wood rotting,
The nettles growing wild.

Where the grass is like a rug,
Spread for a beautiful bug,
And it's all very still,
As you gaze around.

Through that door
Are the skyscrapers and the bungalows
And the streams of cars
And the forest of people of the great city way.

Allen Dart (12)
The Castle School

Young Writers - Poetry In Motion Bristol

The Tiger

The flamingos bask in the morning sun
All prim and proud in their pink costumes.
Rhino remains almost still and silent,
The odd grunt or sigh of weariness.

Then you arrive at the aquarium,
Fish circle continuously never getting dizzy,
Only stopping for breaths of fresh air.
Animal after animal seem dazed or restless.

That's until you get to an enclosure in the far corner,
Here you see a flash of orange every so often,
This wonderful animal is pacing to and fro,
Fury boiling up ready to explode if anyone crossed its path.

Yearning for freedom, back to where it belongs, not this cell.
Where eyes watch your every move,
Where you don't get the satisfaction of killing your own prey.
This strong, powerful, magnificent creature.
The tiger!

Sarah Wyness (13)
The Castle School

My Journey Poem

The cramped, damp and rusty boat lay still,
They all climbed unwillingly and unprepared,
The journey had started, no one knew where it would end.

The waves crashed against the side of the minute boat,
The constant noise of it made people's thoughts unbearable,
The waves whispered a timeless wail that wondered under your soul.

The rats scurried across the rusty boat floor,
As they came close to the Caribbean.
People tried to hold back their fright and tears by biting their lip.

When they got off the boat people got chained around the ankles
And a sign got carved into their hand,
It was a prison bar.

Sabrina Hornby (12)
The Castle School

Prison

They're going to build a prison.

But this is no ordinary prison,
There is no court here,
It is to be a prison of injustice,
Where the convicts are kept behind bars,
Kept behind bars because they are special,
Even though they have done no wrong.

A prison where the secret police bring in with them the stench of
suffering,
A prison where the convicts are exposed to paranoia,
Paranoia, driven by the crowds of mindless people
Staring expressionless.

But beyond this there is hope,
A glimmer of hope in an eye blinded by its own mind,
Blinded by a picture thrust over it so strongly that it cannot see
Reality.
Reality?
Reality that it doesn't want to see,
Reality that is blocked out by this picture.

A picture of happiness and pride,
The vision of somewhere that feels like home,
Warm and free,
Somewhere.
Far, far away.

But as the eye snaps back to reality
It is blinded by something completely different.
Rage.
Rage?
Powered by its only state.
Unhappiness.
Driven by the prison,
Dimly lit and confined.

A prison where the convicts are forced to live in their own world,
Whilst their unsuspecting audience stands and stares,
Whilst life slowly sticks on and the atmosphere dims ever more,
Whilst the convicts' souls slowly slip away,
It is an animal prison,
A 'zoo' they call it,
A place for happiness and enjoyment,
A place supposed to be colourful,
But this is an illusion,
For the convicted animals here,
There isn't even a trace of these things.

This is no life for any animal.

Jed Pietersen (13)
The Castle School

Out Of New York

Out of New York of the dog eating people
Out of New York of the large portion fries
Out of New York of the driving on the other side
Out of New York of the pile-up of yellow
Out of New York still at Ground Zero

Into Bournemouth of living on the beach
Into Bournemouth of the lying in on Sunday
Into Bournemouth the seldom snow town
Into Bournemouth of the blue roof buildings
Into Bournemouth of the fast food orders

Into Bristol the town with no t's
Into Bristol of the just can't be bothered
Into Bristol of the hopping on the bus
Into Bristol of the going down the market
Into Bristol of the always watching tele.

Hannah Shackford (13)
The Castle School

Through That Door . . .

Through that door
Is an angry sea,
A hurricane
Raging furiously.

Where the wind is a monster
Piercing like a knife,
With its threatening howls
Hungry for life.

Through that door
Is a merciless beast,
Reeking pain and havoc,
Its name is Disease.

Where it weaves destruction
Spreading like fire,
Preying on the helpless,
Its appetite will never tire.

Through that door
Is a world of shame,
Where every day's a struggle,
Poverty's to blame.

Where injustice is common
And you can't break free,
Holding you down,
Unforgivingly.

Through that door
Is a battlefield,
Where the soldiers are scarred,
The innocent killed.

With the screech of bombs
As they randomly shatter,
Causing destruction
As if we don't matter.

Through that door
Is a city of sky,
Where dreams reside,
Where angels fly.

Where the clouds form a carpet
Floating so true,
As patient as eternity
Waiting for you . . .

Hattie Bailey (12)
The Castle School

Chimpanzees

The tortoises are motionless in the mysterious darkness,
Stubborn-looking, they slowly get smeared in more and more dirt
As the rain turns up the ground.
Stick insects helplessly frozen in time,
Stiff creatures that resemble dead twigs.

Cautiously and slowly the snakes slither towards each other
Like they are being watched every minute.
They are silent and still as the moon
Like a tiger ready to pounce at any sign of movement.
They are cautious, but blind in this darkness.

Intelligent chimpanzees imprisoned in their cells,
Watching, wondering why me?
Eyes wide, questions being asked constantly.
Crying out to their family observing them through the large black bars.
98% same DNA, our relations and we're responsible.

James Whitbread (13)
The Castle School

Through That Door

Through that door
Are the planets and the stars
Earth, Saturn, Mercury
Jupiter and Mars

Where the planets are balls
Made for you
Some of them
We never knew

Through that door
Are the cactuses and plants
Lots of snakes
And big, large ants

A place that we hate
With no shelter or caves
To protect us from
The hot sunrays

Through that door
Is a world full of fish
Delicious and tasty
In a seafood dish

The king of the mermaids
And his beautiful daughter
Gave me some fish
In a bucket full of water

Through that door
Are the flowers and the trees
Lots of humming
Coming from the honeybees

Where the grass is like a carpet
And the bluebells lie
The wind blowing strong
In the deep blue sky

Through that door
Where the bodies lie
Smelly and rotting
In the midnight sky

Maybe one day
I'll be there
Just like the rest
Life's just not fair.

Sana Ghauri (12)
The Castle School

Nature's Reticence

Have you ever gazed at the sky at night?
Found deep wonders, lost your plight?
Have you ever seen the magic of the moon?
Losing its enchantment if you turn away too soon?

Have you ever wanted to journey through the stars?
Marvelled at the beauty of Venus, Earth and Mars?
Have you ever appreciated the distance of the light?
Have you seen all these wonders in the solitary night?

Sunrise at dawn, sunset at dusk
When the sky is covered with that crimson husk
When all can see nature's true beauty
As the sky continues its timeless duty.

The seagull flaps its wings under the mantle of red
As you lie safely, cosy in your bed
Stop, think, and see my sense
The humble cry of nature's reticence.

Helena Stockwell (14)
The Castle School

Monkey

Sloth high up in his tree
Way up in the Land of Nod
Still as can be
He sleeps

Snake in his ammonite coil
Like a piece of rope
Still as can be
He sleeps

Panda bamboo in hand
Chewing slowly
He boars all around
Whilst wearing a black and white coat

Yet one other creature
Running energetically
Chatting in the sun
With his glossy fur coat

Smart little monkey
Screaming like blue murder
Is a fun little creature
Who interests all that pass by.

Mike McCready (13)
The Castle School

My Journey Poem

France, France, France,
Exotic food, frogs and snails.
'Bonjour, do you like my garlic strings?'
France, France, France,
Friendly, bustling cities.
'Madam, Madam, have a Paris souvenir!'
Out of France.

Into the New Forest, New Forest, New Forest,
Babbling streams and quiet villages,
Empty, idyllic clearings.
New Forest, New Forest, New Forest,
Affectionate, loving wild ponies,
Busy, worn cycle paths being used every day.
Out of the New Forest.

Into Bristol, Bristol, Bristol,
Market stalls everywhere.
'Get your phone covers here, two for £1.50, going cheap, hurry, hurry.'
Bristol, Bristol, Bristol,
Lonely tramps, sitting depressed and sad,
Rain pouring down, car fumes going up and polluting everything.
Out of Bristol.

Emily Ashford (12)
The Castle School

My Journey Poem

South Africa

Onto the plane, away from the penguins waddling on the rocks.
Onto the plane, away from the criminals holding up the banks.
Onto the plane, away from the maids working in the humid heat.
Onto the plane, away from the geckos scrabbling up the side
of an empty swimming pool.

California

Into the airport, to the dry, heat and the white grass.
Into the airport, to the blue sea swarming with surfers.
Into the airport, to the golden beaches and the palm trees.
Into the airport, to the markets covered with curious tourists.

Hungary

Out of the train station, to the mazes of underground walkways.
Out of the train station, to the buffalo tongue and gulyas.
Out of the train station, to the dirty parking lots with gum littering
the ground.
Out of the train station, to the bungalows crouching down next to the
towers of flats.

Emil Lowenberg (12)
The Castle School

Travelling

A loud noise and a puff of smoke
The bustling crowds pushing the people on
Looking out at the horizon
Piling on the fearsome ship
Looking down at the undisturbed water

The deck is empty
The deep blue carrying the ship along
An eerie breeze swishes the ocean
The dark, bottomless water tells travellers beware

As the journey becomes more rocky
People become more chatty
And the misty air thickens
The ships marks footprints on the ocean
Leaving behind chaos

A loud noise and a puff of smoke
The bustling crowds pushing the people off
Looking at the horizon
Piling off the fearsome ship
Looking back at the disturbed water.

Rhiannon Stoate (12)
The Castle School

The Monkey

The sun rises, crowds pile in,
Disappointed, as the animals sleep.
Day after day, the screams, the shouts of excited children
In unbearable heat.

Uneventful iguanas, camouflage themselves
Willing not to be seen or heard.
Grotesque scales help hide him
Until the mass of people are gone.

Gliding through tanks, like a bird through air,
Fish linger in the gloomy water,
As quick as lightning, through the murk,
Short glimpses come, go, are missed.

Through the towering trees, birds are spied,
Crying to be free.
She screams, she shrieks,
Never giving up hope.

Crowds come, hypnotised by an enraged beast,
Imprisoned, he clambers along bars.
The monkey screeches, wails for freedom,
His hot-tempered nature excites his audience.

With boundless energy, he scales the trees,
Swings from rope to rope,
But these are just his dreams, and
He awakes, lonely in his cell.

Once again, the sun will rise,
He's awoken by the noise,
And still he will have to entertain
In a prison he must call home.

Becca North (13)
The Castle School

Holiday Poems

Holland

Travelling along the long flat road
Windmills turning round and round
Not a lot of cars about
Just a load of men on their bicycles
Smoking 'something'
On the way, pretty tulips everywhere
On the way to Amsterdam
Hey, will we ever go *uphill*?

Spain

Ladies dancing with noisy castanets
What a happy feeling
Your skin gets tighter and tighter
Just a bit too much sun I think
Still what a day!
Lovely beaches, warm sea
I'm so happy
Not like that bull in the bull fighting
Afternoons arrive ready for the siesta.

England

I'm standing outside Buckingham Palace
Waiting for a glimpse of royalty
The wind blustering through my ear
I'm so cold, just get me a black cab home
Can't wait to get home to eat those fish and chips
Washed down with a nice cuppa
And then for afters, a nice scone
Mmm!

Louis Osborne (12)
The Castle School

Through That Door

Through that door
Is an exotic location,
The wind is light,
The sky is bright.

Where the rolling sand is like silk
Especially for you,
The trees are luminous,
As you never knew.

Through that door
Is the key to fame,
The smiles of the people,
Just put you to shame.

Lights! Camera! Action!
Shine into the night,
Music blaring,
While they stand in the spotlight.

Through that door
Is my childhood,
My pink teddy,
Look, I'm playing with my friend Eddy.

I'm as small as a mouse
But not as a pea,
I jumped and roared,
I can't believe it's me.

Sarah Huckle (12)
The Castle School

The Lion

The gorilla's sitting around almost dying of boredom
Wondering when will all this end?
The dull grey elephants standing below the cloudy sky
Watching the day go by.
Snakes coiled up hiding from the outside world
Watching and waiting,
For the parents and children to walk on past their large cage.

Then the lion, taking huge strides, walking around with pride
Yet it is sad, for the lion is behind those cold metal bars
Day in, day out.
He hates every day,
Like the fish hate the land.
Its eyes glaring out of the cage thinking of a wilderness of freedom.
He is wondering why it was him they took away from the plain.

He wishes he were there,
He wishes his horrible cage would finally disappear,
He wishes he could take long, endless strides
Across the enormous wilderness.
The crowd stands staring,
At his bushy mane because they are frightened of his power,
They know that the lion could knock anyone of them down
In one single blow.

His paws are enormous and worn out,
He is waiting for the humans to go away from him.
The flies are pestering his strong, tough body.
He is so alone he feels he should die.

Sam Baker (13)
The Castle School

The Panther

The lazy sloth hangs from the branch
Non moving, all seeing, all hearing
Sound and colour move around his form
Frozen in time.

The pig rolls languidly out of the sun
Coarse hair scraping the ground
Spineless ears shade his eyes
Limbs forget moving.

Noses sniff the stifling air
Prairie dogs on watch
Watching for any sign of danger
Watching for *us*.

Yet out of dusky darkness comes
A creature that has not yet forgot
His dreams of moving, running
Beneath *his* swift foot.

He feels not the cement cage floor
Or week-old straw scratching *his* toes
But fresh, clean, soft grass
To *his* mind, *he* is free.

Laura Smith (13)
The Castle School

The Hyena

A solemn grey blanket drawn across the sky,
Unleashing a merciless cascade of watery doom.
Quiet murmuring from the gradual moving hoards
Covered by a sheet of dismal, lifeless umbrellas.

Cumbersome tortoise crawling through bushes,
Rain pelting down on his dull, discoloured shell.
A massive gorilla hauls its immense weight,
Its black bulk matched by the darkened sky.

Winding through long, dense grass,
Lies a snake camouflaged against the green behind,
Meandering peacefully through its cage, like a child's toy,
Calm and gentle, not a vicious menace.

Running to the crowds that watch so eagerly,
Stopping at the fence that holds back freedom,
Then turning and slumping back again,
A hyena patrols the enclosed territory he now owns.

Strolling slowly back and forth,
The ageing rocks at the cage's rear, claimed by more hyenas,
A reminder of their hot homeland,
A place so far from this cold and wet, manmade hell.

Thomas Andrews (13)
The Castle School

Through That Door

Through that door
Is a land of wonder
Full of magic and fantasy
Where I let my mind wander.

Animals with magic powers
That can float in the sky
Dragons of fire, horses with wings
At night to the moon they fly.

Through that door
A secret land of delight
With flowers of many types
And the colours are nice and bright.

A waterfall of beauty
Mystical waters dancing in the stream
Sunlight dancing in the mist
Oh it's a wonderful dream.

Through that door
A night full of stars
That twinkle and shine
I can see as far as Mars.

With space rockets flying
And comets going fast
To the moon you fly
And watch the world go past.

Bobbie-Ann Poulton (12)
The Castle School

Through That Door

Through that door
Is a forest with a pool
With animals, shadows and meadows
Where big trees stand and fall

Where the sun shines
With rain that hails
Dense and dark
Also lots of animals' tails

Through that door
Is a magic place
With lots of faces
Where people are all called 'Mace'

It's a magic place
Where food and water are many
Cold and warm and mild
Where everything costs a penny

Through that door
Is an everlasting sea
Blue and green
It's the place to be

Huge and vast
Very deep and dark
With colourful fish
But also lots of sharks.

Matthew Hooper (12)
The Castle School

Through That Door

Through that door
Is a very dark place
With mice that scurry
And rats that chase.

With its mini streams,
Pipes underground,
Children walking through
Make a terrible sound.

Through that door
Are flowers that bloom,
Children that play
With a dog called Goom.

It has small, little villages,
Birds and bees,
Fruity plants
And cheery trees.

Through that door
Is a planet called Mars,
With little red men
Eating chocolate bars.

With hilly craters
Planet floats in space,
Martians eat dinner,
But first say grace.

Martin Hutton (12)
The Castle School

Through That Door

Through that door
Is Buckingham Palace
With a gold plated ceiling
And a swish carpeted floor.

Where the comfy royal sofas
And the beautiful, glass chandelier
Wait proudly in silence
Like soldiers on duty.

Through that door
Is a tropical beach
With palm trees towering
And exotic flowers blooming.

The ocean washing over
The sandy, golden shore
The pearls of sunshine
Dancing in the light.

Through that door
Is an underwater world
With fishes dancing round
Their beautiful coral maze.

The droplets of tranquillity
Swim through the day
Living in a world
Of magical happiness.

Alice Byrne (12)
The Castle School

Through That Door

Through that door
Is the exotic, tranquil ocean
Complete with nature's harmony
And the waves' rolling motion.

The clear tropical waters
Washed over the golden sand,
The trees that shed the coconuts
Roamed the sunlit land.

Through that door
Is a continent of stars,
Dotted in the deep ebony sky
A stretch of wonders from afar.

As the frosty winter air
Quickened his pace,
The moon shone bright
Down on the globe's windswept face.

Through that door
Was the evidence of fear,
A freeze frame crime
As still as near.

The stench of blood loss
Hung in the tense air,
The drunks in the alley
Staggered away; no reaction, no care.

Heather Sinclair (12)
The Castle School

My World

Through the door
Is the stench of my room
To roam about and discover
Whatever you can find.

All the steamy mist
Blanking the room
Music booming out
Lights flashing through the night.

Through the door
Blankets of sand appear
Soft, hot and wavy sand
Waves splashing up my legs.

Sports playing around
Volleyball over the net
Surfing on the huge waves
Watersports all day long.

Through the door
Out into the busy streets
Cars racing up and down
Revving engines at the ready.

Bags of foods dragged around
Tired faces loafing about
Doors opening and closing
Workers stacking shelves.

Patrick Lines (12)
The Castle School

Through That Door

Through that door
Is a deep blue sky,
The cool wind blowing
As the birds fly by.

With its clouds and mist
A magnificent view
There's a towering mountain
And an ocean too.

Through the door
Is a pitch-black space,
There's nothing there,
It's an empty place.

Beyond Earth's atmosphere,
Surrounded by stars
With its many planets,
Mercury, Venus and Mars.

Through that door
Lies the depths of the sea,
Where the creatures and fish
Drift lazily.

The sun above
Is taking its leave
As through the seaweed
Fishes weave.

Rachel Kwok (12)
The Castle School

Dreams

Through that door
Is the house of my dreams
My own little place
To work and play.

The walls so tall and bright
Surfaces so clean and clear
The carpet soft
Like babies' skin.

Through that door
A balcony full of flowers
So high I feel like I'm flying
I can feel the power.

The beautiful views
Breathtakingly wonderful
Trees and flowers
For as far as the eye can see.

Through that door
Bill, Bob and Joe
My old high school friends
Back together again.

The Little Terrors they called us
Brave and bold
Cool and calm
How I wish it was real.

Sarah Galsworthy (13)
The Castle School

Through That Door

Through that door
Is my imagination.
Everyone was happy
It was such a sensation.

I did not know where to look
Because everyone was so busy.
People were having so much,
I saw a man that was tipsy.

Through that door
Is my worst dream.
Devils with horns,
Things I've never seen.

I was scared,
I could not look.
I saw a man without a hand,
Instead he had a hook.

Through that door
Is what's to come.
I saw a hovercraft in the air,
I thought it looked great fun.

People were wearing silver coats,
I had to wonder why.
I saw a man walking down the street,
And then he began to fly.

Sam Hunt (12)
The Castle School

The Sleep Door

Through that door,
The crazy door,
The door to sleep,
The door that snores.

To the land of dream,
The land of rest,
The land of silence,
The land that's best.

Through that door,
The magic door,
The door of wonder,
Which never bores.

The sight of madness,
The smell of fear,
The taste of nothing,
No road that's clear.

Through that door,
Is endless imagination,
Freeness of mind,
No rules, no nation.

Nick Krupa (12)
The Castle School

The Zoo

A bleak, lifeless world
So empty and confined.
A million times different
From the place they used to call home.

Where crowds wonder endlessly
Around the silent prisons,
They stare, expressionless
Amazed by what they see.

Lions prowl menacingly
Around their cell,
Eyes deeply focused on a far away plain
As it lives this nightmare.

Elephants wallow lazily in the grimy mud
Dreaming of a distant land
Where they are free to do as they please,
A place they call paradise.

The crocodile swaggers awkwardly
Towards the murky water,
Then transforms into a mythical creature
From an ancient land, as it floats along the grubby pool.

Suddenly out of nowhere,
Appear the stars of the show,
The glimmer of light
That is surrounded by an otherwise depressing atmosphere.

The monkeys who entertain us
By performing occasional tricks
Are the resident clowns
Of the zoo.

But this is no life for any animal.

Victoria Piper (14)
The Castle School

Through That Door

Through that door
Is a prehistoric land
Full of dinosaurs, all shapes and sizes
Just desert and sand

A giant T-rex roams the Earth
A stegosaurus with plated armour
A huge long-neck giving birth
The cavemen look like farmers

Through that door
Is a chocolate land
Full of everything you can eat
Different-flavoured sand

A huge mountain of chocolate
A stream of dark Dairy Milk
A massive bowl of white creamy Shot-put
A sticky toffee net of silk.

Gregory Vardon-Smith (13)
The Castle School

The Shark

Millie went for a swim
On the shark in the sea
The fat, fierce, fantastic shark
Followed the fish.

Jessica Watts (13)
Warmley Park Special School